"In this perceptive, thought
Green shows that historic C
panied by an intellectual aw
authentically present, it proves to be intrinsically fruitful for
education because to be a Christian, essentially, is to think as
well as act in a new way. Anti-intellectualism, by contrast, is a
sign that full obedience to the gospel is lacking. Green provides
a very helpful perspective on what has become a central issue
for the church in our time."

David Lyle Jeffrey, Distinguished Professor
of Literature and the Humanities, Baylor University

"Bradley Green poses the question as to why there is so little
written on the relationship between the cross and the life of
the mind. His book is a riveting response to this lack. In an age
when postmodernism seems to have reinforced the oft-held
notions that the human mind and knowledge are unimportant,
we need some guidance on the authentic Christian attitude
toward both. With a focus on creation and the cross, Green's
study looks at the relationship between biblical Christianity and
the human intellectual endeavor. He argues with great clarity
that the postmodern age is no longer interested in knowledge,
and that only by a return to the Christian view of both past and
future can the present have real meaning. This is a much-needed
and timely response to the contemporary *Zeitgeist*."

Graeme Goldsworthy, Visiting Lecturer in Hermeneutics,
Moore Theological College, Sydney, Australia

"*The Gospel and the Mind* gets to the heart of the fact that Christianity is in truth addressed to the human mind, both in its right
ordering and in its critique of a disorder of mind. While keeping
clear the distinction of faith and reason, Christianity has long
sought their proper relationship. There is no belief against mind
and no mind against belief. Bradley Green spells out this tradition
in a welcome reflection on the coherence of Christianity."

James V. Schall, Professor of Political Philosophy,
Georgetown University

"The Enlightenment teaching that reason is a neutral universal act of thought free of tradition has been as decisively refuted as any philosophical theory can be. But the question remains of how to understand the embeddedness of reason in tradition. Professor Green makes a convincing argument that Christianity contains just those foundational beliefs about reality that make the life of the mind possible. Christians who for two centuries have anxiously tried to conform their teachings to Enlightenment reason will discover—perhaps to their astonishment—that it is the gospel that makes reason in its fullest sense possible."

Donald Livingston, Professor of Philosophy,
Emory University

"Readers who take up and read *The Gospel and the Mind* will discover a patient, methodical, and exceedingly well-informed treatise on the intellectual life. Brad Green's book succeeds where many books on the Christian mind or Christian worldview fail. Like Augustine, to whom he regularly returns, Green keeps his sights focused on the beginning and the end and the cross between—on the gospel of Christ and the Christ of the gospel, in whom alone is our hope for renewing the mind."

Peter Leithart, Pastor, Trinity Reformed Church,
Moscow, Idaho; Contributing Editor, *Touchstone*

"Brad Green has written a very accessible book on the intellectual life and its related responsibilities for Christians and the church. He has pursued his central aim by careful appeals to great thinkers in the history of the church: for example, Athanasius, Augustine, and Aquinas. Dr. Green not only grounds his theological work in both creation and the gospel, but also takes on the nihilistic assumptions regarding words and their meaning as espoused in deconstructionism. I gladly commend this work to anyone looking for a clear and thoughtful approach to the church's responsibilities for shaping and preserving the great intellectual traditions so crucial to human flourishing."

Robert B. Sloan Jr., President, Houston Baptist University

"This remarkable and groundbreaking book is an adventure to read. Bradley Green argues convincingly that there is a strong link between Christian faith and the intellectual life of human beings. Given the Christian theological vision of God, human beings, and the world, learning has both a foundation and an animating purpose. Apart from Christian views of creation, history, and redemption, learning is adrift and without ultimate purpose. I strongly recommend this book for all those who long for the recovery of a vibrant intellectual life in our time."

Stephen Davis, Russell K. Pitzer
Professor of Philosophy, Claremont McKenna College

"Brad Green has given us a superb contribution to one of the most important discussions of the new millennium, that of the relation of the head to the heart. His affirmation of the significance of the past and his discussion of a much-neglected feature of the debate—purpose—are particularly worthy aspects of this wide-ranging book. His thorough, though brief, analysis of language and the crucial role it plays in discovering meaning for our lives is one we all need to read. His conclusion is that, ultimately, only an intellect that understands and affirms God's redemption of humanity in Christ will provide a way out of the despair of late modernity."

Drew Trotter, Executive Director,
Consortium of Christian Study Centers

"Brad Green turns relentless scholarship and a forensic eye on a set of controversial questions: Does one's mind matter when it comes to faith? And is it possible not to be a Christian and still have a genuine intellectual life? Contrasting the premodern assumption of the beatific vision with nihilistic modernism, Green makes a compelling case for the necessity of Christianity, both for personal fulfillment and for cultural progress. In the end, Green makes a compelling call for an evangelical reexamination of the need to shape minds in the context of Christ's cross."

Charles T. Evans, Executive Consultant, Paideia, Inc.;
coauthor, *Wisdom and Eloquence:*
A Christian Paradigm for Classical Learning

"I found Brad Green's *The Gospel and the Mind* engaging and helpful. Not another abstract, mind-numbing discussion of 'the Christian mind,' his book is a patient guide for those wanting to deepen their faith. It is a well-reasoned reminder that the true salvation of not only our souls and bodies but also our minds begins at Calvary."

James M. Kushiner, Executive Editor, *Touchstone: A Journal of Mere Christianity*

THE
GOSPEL
AND
THE MIND

RECOVERING AND SHAPING THE INTELLECTUAL LIFE

BRADLEY G. GREEN

WHEATON, ILLINOIS

To
Caleb Conaway Green
Daniel Braun Green
Victoria Glynn Green
Nullus intellectus sine cruce.

The Gospel and the Mind: Recovering and Shaping the Intellectual Life
Copyright © 2010 by Bradley G. Green
Published by Crossway
   1300 Crescent Street
   Wheaton, Illinois 60187

Cover design: Tobias' Outerwear for Books
Cover photo: Wikipedia
Interior design and typesetting: Lakeside Design Plus
First printing 2010
Printed in the United States of America

Unless otherwise indicated, Scripture quotations are from the ESV® Bible (*The Holy Bible, English Standard Version®*), copyright © 2001 by Crossway. Used by permission. All rights reserved.

Scripture quotations marked NASB are from *The New American Standard Bible.®* Copyright © The Lockman Foundation 1960, 1962, 1963, 1968, 1971, 1972, 1973, 1975, 1977, 1995. Used by permission.

All emphases in Scripture quotations have been added by the author.

Trade paperback ISBN:	978-1-4335-1442-5
PDF ISBN:	978-1-4335-1443-2
Mobipocket ISBN:	978-1-4335-1444-9
ePub ISBN:	978-1-4335-2420-2

Library of Congress Cataloging-in-Publication Data
Green, Bradley G., 1965–
   The gospel and the mind : recovering and shaping the intellectual life / Bradley G. Green.
     p. cm.
   Includes bibliographical references and index.
   ISBN 978-1-4335-1442-5 (tp)
   1. Thought and thinking—Religious aspects—Christianity. 2. Intellect—Religious aspects—Christianity. I. Title.
   BV4598.4.G74 2010
   234.01—dc22
                     2010019843

Crossway is a publishing ministry of Good News Publishers.

VP		21	20	19	18	17	16	15	14	13	12	11	10
14	13	12	11	10	9	8	7	6	5	4	3	2	1

Contents

Acknowledgments

There are too many people to thank when one completes a book. My friend Michele Bennett first suggested I contact Crossway. It has been a blessing to work with folks there. Justin Taylor and editor Thom Notaro were professional and helpful through and through. My sincere thanks to all my Crossway friends.

Several friends read all or part of the manuscript and shared their thoughts: Dave Gobbett, Michael Garrett, and Phil Long—I thank you. This manuscript was completed during a research leave granted by my employer, Union University. At Union two colleagues were particularly encouraging as I tried to move this book to completion: my sincere thanks go to Hal Poe and Ray Van Neste. Also, Daryl Charles has been a great encourager of my scholarship. Thanks Daryl.

I cannot imagine a better place to write than Tyndale House (Cambridge, England), where I finished this book while sitting at desk 13, overlooking Selwyn Gardens. I thank Pete Williams and Tyndale friends for a wonderful research leave. I also owe many thanks to friends and

9

acquaintances who took the time to read the manuscript and offer endorsements.

Portions of this book have appeared in print before, if in quite a different form, and are used with permission. Some material came from "Augustine, Modernity, and the Recovery of True Education," *Churchman* (December 2009); "Theological and Philosophical Foundations," in *Shaping a Christian Worldview: The Foundations of Christian Higher Education*, ed. David S. Dockery and Gregory Alan Thornbury (Nashville: Broadman and Holman, 2002). I was writing two chapters for other volumes as I worked on this book, and some ideas from those two chapters, if not text, show up in chapter 6 of this book. Those two chapters are "Colin Gunton and the Theological Origin of Modernity," in *The Theology of Colin Gunton*, ed. Lincoln Harvey (London: T&T Clark, 2010); "Richard Weaver, the Gospel, and the Restoration of Culture," in *Thriving in Babylon: Essays in Honor of A. J. Conyers*, ed. David Capes and J. Daryl Charles (Eugene, OR: Wipf and Stock, 2010).

My family was patient as this book moved closer and closer to completion. I thank Dianne, my wife, and children Caleb, Daniel, and Victoria for their patience as Daddy finished this book. Dianne is patient with me in many things—this book is just one example. Thank you, Dianne. This book is dedicated to Caleb, Daniel, and Victoria. The material may be a little over your heads right now, children, but one day it may be helpful to you. I hope it is.

Introduction

What does the gospel have to do with the life of the mind? Before starting doctoral studies in theology, I had discovered the Reformation, and I suspect every sermon I preached for a year during this time kept circling back to one of Paul's key summaries of the gospel—1 Corinthians 15, where Paul speaks of four *that's* of the gospel: that Christ was killed, that Christ was buried, that Christ arose, that Christ made many appearances. I had discovered precious truths about the gospel of Jesus Christ, and my life would never be the same. I had discovered that the gospel is first and foremost a set of historical events that occurred *outside* of me and *for* me. This gospel, first outside of me, was then applied to me through faith, and I discovered the glory of Christ crucified. I knew that the cross is central to any proper understanding of what it means to be an evangelical. I was not sure, however, how it all might fit together.

Another experience had lodged itself in my head. I had heard D. Bruce Lockerbie speak on a number of occasions. He is fond of saying, "Wherever the gospel is planted, the academy follows."That is, wherever the gospel takes hold of a culture, you inevitably see academies, schools, and institutions of learning develop. They develop not only to teach people how to read and understand the Bible, as important and central as that is. But wherever the gospel goes, it seems to generate intellectual deliberation and inquiry. In one sense this book is an extended effort simply to ask why that is. What is the link between the Christian gospel and intellectual deliberation, between the Christian faith and learning? Why has the Christian faith always seemed to spur on the intellectual life? What is the connection, indeed, between the gospel and the mind?

As a father of (then) an infant, I had dreamed of what kind of education I wanted to offer my child. I began to get to know new friends and colleagues at Union University while completing my PhD (that dissertation still had to be finished), and some of us began to dream about starting a school for our children and other children in the community. As I wrestled with how to articulate the Christian theological moorings of education, I read Colossians 1:15ff., particularly verses 21–22: "And you, who once were alienated and hostile in mind, doing evil deeds, he has now reconciled in his body of flesh by his death, in order to present you holy and blameless and above reproach before him."

Two interrelated truths impressed themselves upon my mind: (1) our alienation and hostility toward God as sinners includes the alienation and hostility of our *minds*; (2) it is through the cross that this alienation and hostility are overcome. As I thought through this, I realized that the seeds of a radically *evangelical* approach to the intellectual life were present. If in his death Christ redeemed *all* of who we are, that must include our intellectual life. Christ did not die to redeem *part* of us, but he died to redeem all of who we are—including our minds.

In one sense this monograph is an attempt to explicate this fundamental insight and to wrestle with the question, what does the gospel have to do with the intellectual life? Hence the main title of this book, *The Gospel and the Mind*, comes from my interest in exploring the relationship between the atonement and the life of the mind, an interest triggered at least in part by meditating on Colossians 1:21–22. The outline of this book was essentially generated in an afternoon at my office at Union University. However, the argument of the book extends beyond the question of the cross (narrowly considered) to include five main interrelated Christian theological themes and their relevance to the intellectual life:

1. The realities of creation and history
2. The notion of a telos or goal to all of history
3. The cross of Christ
4. The nature of language
5. Knowledge, morality, and action

Augustine (354–430) once wrote that he had come to understand what he believed through the process of writing: "I must also acknowledge, incidentally, that by writing I have myself learned much that I did not know."[1] As I have read and written and rewritten, two main interlocking theses have emerged, and these two theses function as the heart and soul of this book: (1) the Christian vision of God, man, and the world provides the necessary precondition of the recovery of any meaningful intellectual life; (2) the Christian vision of God, man, and the world offers a particular, unique

---

[1] Augustine, *The Trinity*, trans. Edmund Hill, The Works of Saint Augustine (Brooklyn, NY: New City, 1991), 3.1.

understanding of what the intellectual life might look like. As I wrote and rewrote, I found myself at first thinking I was just arguing the first thesis—the Christian vision of things provides the necessary precondition for the life of the mind. But the more I wrote, I realized that a complementary (and interlocking) thesis was emerging—the Christian vision of things offers a particular understanding and construal of the life of the mind.

In writing a book on the Christian mind, I am all too conscious of my own shortcomings. For my defense, I take my cue from Dorothy Sayers. Toward the beginning of her seminal essay on education and potential education reform, "The Lost Tools of Learning," Sayers concedes that her critics might ask why she has any authority to hold forth on education. Her answer is simple. Though not a formal educator, she was a student her whole life, much of it spent in formal education.[2] As someone who invested much of her life in schooling, she was confident she had at least *some* authority to speak on the matter.

I likewise have spent many years in school. And I have been teaching at various levels for some twelve years. Like many students, I came to value education much later in the game than is wise. While gaining this appreciation certainly was a process, looking back I seem to have realized abruptly that something was wrong. Why were so many historical events, so many older authors, so many seminal texts and works foreign to me? I suspect that I wasn't the only young person who would find himself at a dinner party or conference, nodding in agreement with others' observations, posing with a knowing look while asking

---

[2] Dorothy Sayers, "The Lost Tools of Learning." This essay has been reprinted numerous times. Many first read it in *National Review* in 1948. It has been reprinted in *Education in a Free Society*, ed. Anne Husted Burleigh (Indianapolis: Liberty Fund, 1973), and as an appendix to Douglas Wilson, *Recovering the Lost Tools of Learning* (Wheaton, IL: Crossway, 1991).

myself, "Now who *was* Anselm, and *which* century did he live in?" As I have wrestled with the realization that I indeed missed something along the way, I have tried both to rectify my own situation and so to act and live that things will be different for my children and other children in my community.

Having gone through school and now made the transition to teaching at a small liberal arts college, I have discovered that others have had similar experiences. They have come to the realization that they really have missed something crucial in their education. And it is important to emphasize that this is not simply the mature act of realizing that our knowledge is minuscule compared to all there is to know. What I am speaking of is not simply a humility that comes with age. I am describing a more troubling reality among my contemporaries marked by a genuine ignorance of the past, a lack of grounding in the cultural and intellectual inheritance of the West, and perhaps most sadly, no sort of remorse or recognition that this situation might be a bad thing.

In the end, Aldous Huxley's vision in *Brave New World* might be truer to reality than George Orwell's *1984* or Ray Bradbury's *Fahrenheit 451*. In *1984* and *Fahrenheit 451* some people develop a passion or concern for what is right and for not succumbing to the forces that would rob them of their dignity and purpose as human beings. But Huxley may indeed be more accurate: in *Brave New World* there is very little genuine concern about how culture and society have developed. The fact that the state is all-encompassing and all-controlling, and that a scientific worldview permeates the culture, is of little concern to most characters in the novel. The great majority of them are no longer living, in one sense, in that they have given up (if even unwittingly) on any sort of truly meaningful life.[3]

This book perhaps has its origin in my own theological studies at seminary and later at a university. I was simultaneously wrestling with *modern* skepticism about the possibility of knowledge—whether of God or otherwise—and with so-called *postmodern* skepticism of or challenges to knowledge. While I have since come to the conviction that the modern and so-called postmodern challenges are cut from the same cloth, these challenges set me on a course from which I have ultimately never departed.[4] During and since my formal time of study, those challenges have always been in the back of my mind. Part of what this book attempts to do is to answer those legitimate questions and challenges, and I have attempted to do so by arguing that it is the Christian vision (and, ultimately, only the Christian vision of God, man, and the world) that provides the necessary substructure, or precondition, for meaningful and enduring *intellectus* (understanding).

One of the Christian faith's great insights is that nothing lies outside the good and providential workings of God. This includes the life of the mind. Indeed, some of the church's earliest and most profound thinkers were making the connection between the reality of God and the possibility of human understanding. For example, Origen (born ca. AD 185) wrote:

> Truly He is that light which illuminates the whole understanding of those who are capable of receiving truth, as is said in Psalms 36, "In Thy light we shall see light." For what other

---

[3] Is my concern an ancient concern as well? In the *Republic*, is Plato saying the same thing in his analogy of the cave? He is trying to convince his friends that there is something greater that they must embrace. His friends are blind to reality and have yet to see.

[4] See A. J. Conyers, "Is Postmodernism a Helpful Matrix for Theology?" *Christian Scholar's Review* 33, no. 3 (Spring 2004): 293–309.

light of God can be named, "in which any one sees light," save
an influence of God, by which a man, being enlightened, either
thoroughly sees the truth of all things, or comes to know God
Himself, who is called the truth: Such is the meaning of the
expression, "In Thy light we shall see light"; i.e., in Thy word
and wisdom which is Thy Son, in Himself we shall see Thee the
Father. Because He is called light, shall He be supposed to have
any resemblances to the light of the sun? Or how should there
be the slightest ground for imagining, that from the corporeal
light any one could derive the cause of knowledge, and come
to the understanding of the truth?[5]

Similarly, Origen says that God "is the mind and source from
which all intellectual nature or mind takes its beginning."[6]
Indeed, Origen argues that as image bearers we are shaped
in such a way that knowledge of divine things is possible.[7]

In stark contrast to the Christian tradition, the modern
age—which has often constricted itself to seeing knowledge
as chiefly available through the senses—has often balked
at affirming the possibility of knowledge of the supernatural, or suprasensible reality. But as Origen wrote, "It is one
thing to see, and another to know: to see and to be seen is a
property of bodies; to know and to be known, an attribute
of intellectual being."[8]

Origen, like Augustine who will follow him, construes
the intellectual life in theological, indeed christological,
terms. Thus, Origen quotes John 1:9 regarding Jesus, "He
is the true light, which enlightens every man that cometh
into this world." And referring to Matthew 11:27, Origen
speaks of Christ as "the image by which we come to the

[5]Origen On First Principles 1.1.1 (Anti-Nicene Fathers, vol. 4, ed. Alexander Roberts and James
Donaldson [Peabody, MA: Hendrickson, 1994], 242).
[6]Ibid., 1.1.6.
[7]Ibid., 1.1.7.
[8]Ibid.

knowledge of the Father, whom no one knows save the Son, and he to whom the Son is pleased to reveal Him." Origen continues, "The method of revealing Him is through the understanding."[9]

What I am trying to do in this work might best be portrayed in contradistinction to two brief statements in Roger Scruton's book *An Intelligent Person's Guide to Modern Culture*. In the preface Scruton summarizes his project succinctly: "Culture, I suggest, has a religious root and a religious meaning. This does not mean that you have to be religious in order to be cultivated. But it does mean that the point of being cultivated cannot, in the end, be explained without reference to the nature and value of religion."[10] And in his "Conclusions" he says, "Culture is rooted in religion, and . . . the true effort of a high culture is to perpetuate the common culture from which it grew—to perpetuate it not as religion, but as art, with the ethical life transfixed within the aesthetic gaze."[11]

Scruton recognizes that cultural development and sustenance have a religious root. There is something about religious conviction (or at least about some religious convictions) that is inextricably tied to cultural development. Indeed, wherever the cross is planted the academy follows. Scruton is happy to cut the Gordian knot and say that one can actually have the cultural development without the religious root itself.[12] One of the key burdens of this book

---

[9]Ibid., 1.2.6.
[10]Roger Scruton, *An Intelligent Person's Guide to Modern Culture* (South Bend, IN: St. Augustine's Press, 2000), x.
[11]Ibid., 149.
[12]The "Gordian knot" imagery comes from the life of Alexander the Great. Upon entering the town of Gordium, Alexander was shown the wagon upon which Midas had purportedly entered the town. Apparently a prophecy had declared that whoever could untie the intricate knot by which a yoke was attached to the wagon would thereby be granted the right to rule all of Asia. Alexander, after attempting to untie the knot (and finding it nigh impossible), simply took out his sword and cut the rope below the knot. Hence, to "cut the Gordian knot" is shorthand for a determined, if violent (and possibly unethical) way to accomplish one's aim.

is to suggest that *without certain key theological realities and commitments, the cultivation of an enduring intellectual and cultural life becomes increasingly difficult, if not impossible.*

In short, there is an inseparable relationship between the reality of the gospel and the cultivation of the intellectual life. When the gospel ceases to permeate and influence a given culture, we often see a confused understanding of the possibility of knowledge and the meaning of our thoughts. Ultimately, where the gospel is not holding sway, it should not surprise us to see the subtle or not-so-subtle disintegration of, or rejection of, meaningful intellectual engagement and activity.

A number of recent works have explored similar territory, some from more and some from less explicitly Christian theological moorings. For example, in his recent book *Education's End*, Anthony T. Kronman laments that colleges and universities have "given up on the meaning of life."[13] C. John Sommerville, in his recent book *The Decline of the Secular University*, takes aim at the secularism of the contemporary university and offers an argument for the necessity of religion. Sommerville observes, "Universities are not giving us much practice at formulating worldviews, in [their] haste to fit us for our jobs."[14] The thesis of the present monograph has some kinship to Sommerville's work. Sommerville repeats the lament of Clark Kerr, former president of the California university system, who says that universities have "no great vision to lure them on, only the need for survival."[15]

---

[13]Anthony T. Kronman, *Education's End: Why Our Colleges and Universities Have Given Up on the Meaning of Life* (New Haven: Yale University Press, 2007).
[14]C. John Sommerville, *The Decline of the Secular University* (Oxford: Oxford University Press, 2006), 14.
[15]Ibid., 21. Sommerville is quoting David L. Kirp, *Shakespeare, Einstein, and the Bottom Line* (Cambridge, MA: Harvard University Press, 2003), 259.

This lack of vision will occupy us in the second chapter. True education requires an animating and inspiring vision, which is the very thing the gospel provides, and which is the very thing missing in most construals of education today. I particularly resonate with Sommerville when he writes of "the intellectual void that results when religious categories are systematically rejected."[16] I will be arguing that the Christian vision of God, man, and the world provides the most meaningful and coherent presuppositional framework for the intellectual life. Again, Sommerville is correct when he writes that "the academy needs to learn to speak theologically."[17] All intellectual discourse is—at a very fundamental level—theological, and the failure to appreciate this has most certainly led Christian thinkers and intellectuals to construe their own intellectual and academic endeavors in ways that are not as theologically robust as they should be.

Oliver O'Donovan notes that many Western cultural institutions persist even though we have no idea why we should show allegiance to them: "So Western civilization finds itself the heir of political institutions and traditions which it values without any clear idea why, or to what extent, it values them."[18] In an analogous way, we are accustomed to believing that knowledge, meaning, and communication should all be affirmed as real and important, but we may not always draw the connection that all of these realities—in some way, shape, or form—are ultimately defensible only in the light of the vision of God, man, and the world that the Christian faith provides.

---

[16]Ibid., 24.
[17]Ibid., 32.
[18]Oliver O'Donovan, *The Ways of Judgment*, The Bampton Lectures 2003 (Grand Rapids: Eerdmans, 2005), xiii.

Thus Robert W. Jenson can speak of "the—barely—existing intellectual world."[19] In commenting on Allan Bloom's book *The Closing of the American Mind*, Jenson says, "The nation built on Enlightenment has not merely become ignorant and unthinking, or even anti-intellectual in Richard Hofstadter's sense, but is becoming incapable of thought."[20] *Incapable of thought.* It is the purpose of this book to tease out Jenson's insight. Is there a connection between the loss of the gospel's hold on the modern world and the modern world's increasing skepticism about the viability, purpose, meaning, and possibility of an intellectual life? Again, out of this question emerge the two theses of the book summarized above:

1. The Christian vision of God, man, and the world provides the necessary precondition for the recovery of any meaningful intellectual life.
2. The Christian vision of God, man, and the world offers a particular, unique understanding of what the intellectual life might look like.

Jenson also writes, "It is the insight of the whole line from Rousseau to Nietzsche that reason undoes itself because it undoes God, without whom reason—as every other interesting virtue—is groundless. . . . The university is to be democracy's temple, but it is to house no God."[21] Jenson's thesis forms the backdrop of this book—"reason undoes itself because it undoes God." As the gospel loses hold on a culture—or as people lose hold of the gospel—the rationale for the use of reason (and the intellectual life

---

[19]Robert W. Jenson, "On the Renewing of the Mind: Reflections on the Calling of Christian Intellectuals," in *Essays in Theology of Culture* (Grand Rapids: Eerdmans, 1995), 171.
[20]Ibid., 164.
[21]Ibid., 165.

more broadly) becomes inexplicable. Noting the decline of the liberal arts in American institutions of higher learning, Jenson comments, "It seems likely that the liberal character of America's colleges stands and falls with their ideologically and liturgically Christian character."[22] Hence, we should not be surprised to see in our own day (and we have seen it for some time) an increasing confusion about the possibility of the intellectual life and a jaded cynicism or flippancy about the importance and possibility of knowledge.

Jenson has argued in a way similar to how I am arguing here. In a culture denuded of anything meaningful in the *public* square, people will turn to an endless variety of things to find meaning in the *private* realm. Thus Jenson writes, "It is no accident at all that mystery-cults and esoteric wisdoms flourish in California or Minneapolis as once in old Corinth or Alexandria." But it is his next statement that most resonates with the line of argument I am advancing: "Neither is it an accident that the *liberal* arts languish."[23]

As we will later see, Jenson argues that the liberal arts are most fully realized in ecclesial settings, or at least in settings where the church is vibrant and fulfilling her calling. Thus the Greeks could hear "the gospel as a promise that specific humanity, just as Athens had evoked it, was not a delusion, and they could see the church as a community in which specific humanity could occur."[24] Likewise, "where freedom is abstract and arbitrary, and needs no community, neither does it need arts. It is again no accident that where historical relativism rules, the liberal arts die."[25] Jenson concludes, "The gospel gives hope for the freedom that the liberal arts

---

[22]Robert W. Jenson, "Hope, the Gospel, and the Liberal Arts," in *Essays in Theology of Culture*, 180.
[23]Ibid., 184.
[24]Ibid., 185.
[25]Ibid., 188.

serve. The liberal arts give hope that the free person whom the gospel evokes can actually exist."[26]

In a related essay Jenson argues: "If scholars of the liberal arts wish to pursue and maintain their calling, they must emulate the church's use of Scripture. If they will not, it is likely that the process now so far along will grind to its completion and the liberal arts will disappear altogether." In fact, "the church has throughout the history of our culture been in its communal entity the very *possibility* of the liberal arts."[27] Jenson argues further:

> If an academic institution is to teach the liberal arts, it must embrace within its cognitive grasp Aristotle and Isaiah and Machiavelli and Luther and the future genius who will yet unify field theory, as partners of a single continuing conversation that is identical with its own single communal reality. That it can do only by faith in the unity of truth, which is to say, in God.[28]

For Jenson the loss of the viability and apparent coherence of the liberal arts is tied to the loss of trust in the "narrativity of history." And this loss of trust in the "narrativity of history" is rooted in "the more general loss of confidence that there is a total narrative, an encompassing universal history, a tale to be told about the first beginning and about the last end and about the way from one to the other."[29]

---

[26]Ibid., 189. The end of this essay has a passage worth quoting at length: "The mere practice itself becomes a spring of hope. Folk who labor on great inherited texts as if they matter liberate all around them to confidence that history does have some plot. Those who practice the arts of public discourse open little polities just by doing so, each time they break the silence. Those who discipline themselves to the outcome of experiment and observation, when they do it for the sake of truth, encourage all to faith that there *is* truth. To pursue beauty is to create it for all to see and hear. When we act as if human deliberation and decision could make a difference, they *do* make a difference. When we act as if community were real, it just thereby *becomes* real" (189).
[27]Robert W. Jenson, "God, the Liberal Arts, and the Integrity of Texts," in *Essays in the Theology of Culture*, 212.
[28]Ibid., 213.
[29]Ibid., 214.

Ultimately, you cannot affirm the reality of an overarching narrative encompassing all reality unless you can affirm the reality of God. In short, "there are presently few if any ways for a collective—such as a college—to hold on to its own narrativity except by worshipping the church's God."[30]

Like Jenson, I will maintain that the intellectual life truly makes sense only in light of the realities of the Christian vision of God, man, and the world. A sustainable and meaningful life of the mind will prosper and grow only in soil nurtured by such a Christian vision.

Dallas Willard offers a penetrating critique of how a belief in knowledge holds no real place in the contemporary university. According to Willard, a cluster of "secular myths" has coalesced over time to squeeze out the notion that the Bible is a legitimate source of knowledge. Ultimately these secular myths have rendered meaningless the notion of any legitimate knowledge whatsoever. Willard briefly traces the history of knowledge. At one point *authority* was central to how people obtained knowledge, then *reason* was central, and finally *sense experience*. When sense experience became central, the "scientific method" was more and more seen as the main or only way of knowing. Since key Christian affirmations about God, man, the world, and the relationships that link all of these are generally *not* observable by sense experience, the claims of theology or religion were seen to be outside the purview of true knowledge. As a result, Willard writes, "The heart of the university crisis is, in my view, *the simple fact that its institutional structures and processes are no longer organized around knowledge.*"[31]

[30]Ibid.
[31]Dallas Willard, "The Unhinging of the American Mind: Derrida as Pre-Text," in *European Philosophy and the American Academy*, ed. Barry Smith, Monist Library of Philosophy (LaSalle, IL: Hegeler Institute, 1994), 3. Emphasis mine.

Willard's point regarding the expulsion of the biblical text from the university is that, while secular myths cannot justify the reality of knowledge or answer the key questions of human existence (Who are we? What is good? How do we become good?), the Christian narrative can. Much as Willard is arguing that the secular vision of the world cannot justify the existence of, or quest for, knowledge, I am arguing here that the Christian vision of God, man, and the world provides the necessary precondition for recovering any meaningful intellectual life.[32]

Similarly, an older essay by Josef Pieper raises questions about what we currently call science, but we could easily expand his discussion to include other intellectual disciplines. Pieper suggests that science can live and prosper and develop only when it is related to a larger understanding of reality—that is, only within a certain vision of the nature of things. He writes that science "would necessarily lose its legitimacy and inherent credibility as soon as it was severed from its origin, namely, from the foundation of that total worldview. Just such a separation, I hold, occurred at the inception of the modern era."[33] At the end of his book *Abuse of Language, Abuse of Power*, Pieper comes close to the heart of my concern. True learning—and Pieper is speaking of one component of true learning, "freedom of science"—requires for its survival a certain rootedness in a vision and understanding of reality: "The notion 'freedom of science' springs, perhaps unexpectedly, from very deep roots indeed, and . . . the radical challenge we have to face nowadays demands a defense aware of these roots."[34]

---

[32]Dallas Willard, *The Bible and the University*, Scripture and Hermeneutics Series 8 (Grand Rapids: Zondervan, 2007).
[33]Josef Pieper, *Abuse of Language, Abuse of Power*, trans. Lothar Krauth (1974; repr., San Francisco: Ignatius, 1988), 47.
[34]Ibid., 54.

Indeed, in the Western world there is a rich tradition emphasizing the life of the mind. Much of that emphasis flows from our Christian inheritance, as seen in the biblical documents and in key thinkers of the West (Augustine, Anselm, Aquinas, Calvin, among others). As the modern world has jettisoned its Christian intellectual inheritance, there has been a corresponding confusion about the value of the mind, even of the possibility of knowledge at all, whether of God or of the created order.

This book suggests that a return to the most promising life of the mind is ultimately a return to a life grounded in Christ and the cross, and in the larger Christian vision of things, where the gospel is central. The following chapters retrieve central themes of the West's Christian inheritance and suggest that such themes form the matrix of any promising and sustainable intellectual life.

In chapter 1, I suggest that whereas modern thinkers often are skeptical about the importance of knowledge and about a real order of things, Christian thinkers have affirmed that the created order is truly that, a created order. Intellectual life therefore comes in contact with "the truth of things," to use Aquinas's words. The doctrine of creation allowed premodern thinkers to affirm that education, or the life of the mind, is not primarily about constructing knowledge or imposing order, but about receiving knowledge, about discovering what is already there. A corollary of the importance of creation is the fact that Christians have always given attention to the past, to *history*, because the Christian faith is a historical faith where past events shape the present and the future, and because Christians (at their best) recognized that knowledge is often mediated to us in that it comes from outside us and from the past.

In chapter 2, I submit that whereas much of modern thought appears to be adrift with no direction or purpose, premodern Christian thinkers almost always engaged in intellectual endeavors against the backdrop of an overarching telos or goal. The telos of the vision of God was the goal that animated and informed Augustine's intellectual deliberations and the medieval tradition that followed him. Interestingly, this larger telos both *exalted* the importance of the life of the mind by seeing it as part of a larger and grander picture of the world and *humbled* the life of the mind by recognizing that intellectual life is not simply its own end, but serves a larger goal—the glory and vision of God.

In chapter 3, I maintain that while modern thinkers have often construed the life of the mind as a morally neutral reality, severed from the heart and will, the best of Christian thought has always recognized that the life of the mind is a gracious gift, is a part of the whole life of the person, and must always serve larger purposes than simply the acquisition of facts. On a Christian understanding, it is the cross of Christ that frees the mind to truly think God's thoughts after him and to submit our thoughts to the universal lordship of Christ. This is perhaps best seen in Jesus' command to love God with our minds, in Paul's teaching that Christians are to take every thought captive to the obedience of Christ, and in Augustine's and Anselm's teaching of "faith seeking understanding," which holds that true understanding is always rooted in a previous faith commitment to the Mind behind all knowledge.

In chapters 4 and 5, I contend that whereas the modern world is bewildered about the nature of language and the possibility of meaning in communication, the Christian tradition affirms a rich theology of language and communication. Words and signs are meaningful because they are part of a created order, because man as image bearer is a communicating and relational being, and because words and signs exist in relation to the Word (i.e., Christ), who serves as the ground and goal of all language.

In chapter 6, I suggest that knowledge in the modern world is often seen as morally neutral and is also often severed from any inherent relationship to practice. A Christian understanding of the intellectual life must take into account—contrary to the typical modern understanding—the inherently moral nature of knowledge, the way knowledge is linked to the heart and will of the knower, and how the best of Christian thought has virtually always affirmed the necessary and inseparable connection between knowledge and practice.

In sum, the way forward entails attention to the past. A recovery of a genuine and meaningful life of the mind is ultimately a recovery of Christ and the gospel. In such a recovery of the essentials of Christianity we find the true and enduring foundation for the intellectual life.

It is not the remembered but the forgotten past that enslaves us. . . . To study the past does indeed liberate us from the present, from the idols of our own market-place. But I think it liberates us from the past too.

C. S. LEWIS

The natural world around us can be empirically known precisely because it has first been "thought" by the Creator.

JOSEF PIEPER

We never wonder quite enough at the fact that scientific knowledge is possible at all.

LOUIS DE BROGLIE

Our fundamental beliefs are . . . basic acts of acknowledgement in response to some intelligibility inherent in the nature of things.

THOMAS F. TORRANCE

1

Creation and the Importance of the Past

Is there anything unique to our time, or more broadly to the modern age in general, that might help to explain the inchoate and stilted life of the mind that characterizes our age? In this chapter I will suggest that much of our modern dilemma—our confusion about the possibility and nature of true knowledge—is rooted in a poor understanding of two interrelated issues: history and creation. These two realities are intricately related as both come to us from outside of us and resist human manipulation. History and creation remind us that some things simply *are* and have their existence apart from our wills and intellect. I will attempt to show that confused or inadequate understandings of history and creation contribute to the kind of culture and ethos that does not value the intel-

31

lectual life. I will also try to show that the life of the mind is ultimately dependent on a certain understanding of history and creation, and—in turn—that Christianity provides profound, compelling teaching on the centrality of history and creation. We begin with creation.

The Centrality of Creation

Any genuine affirmation of the importance of education as centered on knowledge of what is truly *there* must be rooted in a doctrine of creation. Jean Daniélou has written, "Truth consists in the intelligence's conforming itself to this order . . . . [Intelligence] consists in knowing reality as it is."[1] Thus Thomas Aquinas speaks similarly of coming into contact with "the truth of things."[2] Richard Weaver adds, "Our conception of metaphysical reality finally governs our conception of everything else, and, if we feel that creation does not express purpose, it is impossible to find an authorization for purpose in our lives."[3]

Lying behind this whole way of thinking is an understanding of creation. When we see the world as a fundamentally good reality, there is an impetus to understand the world. When the world is seen as fundamentally bad, there is an impetus to ignore it. And I will suggest that a denial of the notion of creation not only discourages sustained attention to the world, but similarly discourages sustained attention to

---

[1] Jean Daniélou, *The Scandal of Truth* (1962), 8, quoted in David Lyle Jeffrey, "Knowing Truth in the Present Age," *Crux* 34, no. 2 (June 1998), 23.
[2] This terminology is common in Thomas. For example: "Now it is the property of wisdom that through it one may have a right judgment about things. But he judges rightly about the truth of things who can discern how someone deviating from the truth is deceived; therefore, to show that in God there is wisdom, he adds *He himself knows both the deceiver and the one who is being deceived*, that is, by right judgment He discerns the deceptions by which someone misses the truth from the right knowledge of the truth." Thomas Aquinas, *The Literal Exposition of Job: A Scriptural Commentary Concerning Providence*, chap. 12 (208), accessed in *The Collected Works of St. Thomas Aquinas* (Past Masters, InteLex).
[3] Richard Weaver, *Ideas Have Consequences* (Chicago: University of Chicago Press, 1948), 51.

the past—what has come before. It is worth noting that non-Christian intellectuals have at times recognized the possibility that meaning is ultimately rooted in a doctrine of creation. One particularly bold critic of historic Christian orthodoxy, Friedrich Nietzsche (1844–1900), has written: "The presuppositions that things are, at bottom, ordered so morally that human reason must be justified—is an ingenuous presupposition and a piece of naiveté, the after-effect of belief in God's veracity—God understood as the creator of things."[4] Albert Einstein is quoted as saying, "The belief in an external world independent of the perceiving subject is the basis of all natural science."[5] In response to this, Thomas F. Torrance suggests that "somehow there is 'a pre-established harmony' between human thought and independent empirical reality, in virtue of which the human mind can discern and grasp the relational structures embedded in nature."[6]

At the heart of historic Christian orthodoxy is the affirmation that we live in a created world. In identifying the Christian God, the Nicene and Apostles' Creeds speak of "God, the Father Almighty, maker of heaven and earth." Scripture is clear that God created all things and that he did so out of nothing (Genesis 1–2; Psalm 33; John 1:3; Acts 17:24–25; Col. 1:16; Heb. 1:3). This good world was created freely by a good God, who was under no compulsion or necessity. The historic Christian doctrine of creation *ex nihilo* ("out of nothing") is central to an understanding of the intellectual life for several

---

[4]Friedrich Nietzsche, *The Will to Power*, trans. Walter Kaufmann and R. J. Hollingdale (New York: Vintage, 1968), 262.
[5]Quoted in Thomas F. Torrance, *Christian Theology and Scientific Culture* (Belfast: Christian Journals, 1980), 57–58, cited by Douglas F. Kelly, "The Realist Epistemology of Thomas F. Torrance," in *An Introduction to Torrance Theology: Discovering the Incarnate Saviour*, ed. Gerritt Scott Dawson (London: T&T Clark, 2007), 99.
[6]Torrance, *Christian Theology and Scientific Culture*, 58, quoted in Kelly, "The Realist Epistemology of Thomas F. Torrance," 100.

important reasons. First, there is a "givenness" to things with which the Christian must come to terms. There is indeed a reality outside of the human person, and man finds himself in a world not of his own making.[7] Thus, while man is certainly given dominion over the world in Genesis 1:26ff., this dominion is over something that already *is*. He is not called to manipulate things however he wishes. Rather, he is called to work with and shape and rule over things as they are already structured, already constituted in *this* way and not *that*. Thus, from the very beginning of his existence man has found himself in relation to the rest of the created order with its built-in structure, which we all must recognize and respect.

Humanity is often at odds with the created order and has articulated this animosity in stunningly clear ways. Karim Rashid is a contemporary designer whose work—from chairs, to garbage cans, to saltshakers—has generated a cult following of sorts. Some museums even feature his creations in their displays. Rashid offers a striking example of man's desire to kick against the created order. He explains why he disliked being outdoors as a child: "I didn't like nature because it was already done. It was designed. You couldn't do anything to it."[8]

---

[7] I would thus argue that a Christian doctrine of creation requires a realist, rather than an antirealist, view of how we relate to the world. Simply put, realism affirms that there is an external (to me) world that exists independent of my thoughts and/or experience. Antirealism affirms that the external world is dependent on my thoughts and/or experience. See Keith Yandell, "Modernism, Post-Modernism, and the Minimalist Canons of Common Grace," *Christian Scholar's Review* 27 (Fall 1997): 15–26.

[8] Rob Brinkley, "Karim Rashid," *American Way*, June 15, 2004, 62. Rashid may be guilty of a complex error, perhaps a double error. First, Rashid errs in not affirming the fundamental goodness and rightness of the structures inherent in the created order. Second, and more tragically, God has not called Rashid (or anyone else) simply to look at a "done" creation in relation to which no action could or should be taken. Rather, God calls Rashid (and us all) to exercise dominion over an already *good* creation, and to transform it in accord with the rest of Scripture, while never forgetting that fundamental goodness of the creation *as* creation.

Second, the doctrine of creation implies that there is indeed something that can be known. There is a real world, and what we see around us is not simply a fantasy or an illusion (as some Eastern religions profess). Rather, this world is truly *there* (or *here*), and it can be encountered and known. The world is not chaos or a random association of stuff. It is an ordered reality, and when Christians further affirm that God is a *speaking* God who has created us as *knowing* creatures, there is powerful theological grounding for the possibility of knowledge.

Richard Weaver suggests that the idea that there is a world of truth "worth knowing and even worth reverencing" ultimately requires a doctrine of creation:

> Clearly this [i.e., that there is a body of data worth knowing] presumes a certain respect for the world as creation, a belief in it and a trust in its providence, rather than a view (as if out of ancient Gnosticism) positing its essential incompleteness and badness. The world is there a priori; the learner has the duty of familiarizing himself with its nature and its set of relations.[9]

The psalmist makes this point vividly:

> When I look at your heavens, the work of your fingers,
> the moon and the stars, which you have set in place . . .
> (Ps. 8:3)

Consider, as well, Psalm 19:1–2:

> The heavens declare the glory of God,
> and the sky above proclaims his handiwork.
> Day to day pours out speech,
> and night to night reveals knowledge.

---

[9]Richard M. Weaver, *Visions of Order: The Cultural Crisis of Our Time* (1964; repr., Wilmington, DE: Intercollegiate Studies Institute, 1995), 126.

As Marion Montgomery suggests (borrowing a phrase from Aquinas), education is concerned with coming in contact with "the truth of things."[10] A Christian view of knowledge is therefore concerned not simply with the world of speculation, but rather with the world *as it is*. Thus, Josef Pieper, following Aquinas, can say that "the essence of knowing would lie, not in the effort of thought as such, but in the grasp of the being of things, in the discovery of reality."[11]

Richard Weaver was a particularly astute critic of modernity, and we will find ourselves benefitting from his insights in these pages. Weaver suggests that much of modern educational theory is ultimately gnostic. He means two things by his charge of gnosticism: (1) creation is inherently evil, the work of a demiurge limited in power; (2) man does not require salvation from outside himself, but is already in a state of "Messianic blessedness."[12] Gnosticism, according to Weaver, "is a kind of irresponsibility—an irresponsibility to the past and to the structure of reality in the present."[13] Gnosticism fails because its advocates, on Weaver's understanding, "are out of line with what is."[14] Gnosticism errs on several fronts.

First, whereas gnosticism predicates evil of the world itself, Christianity sees a good world that is now caught up in the sin of fallen human beings. Second, whereas gnosticism sees evil and chaos in the world from the beginning, Christianity sees a good, ordered world that

---

[10]Historic Christianity roots the "truth of things" in the fact that we live in a good, created, and orderly world. See Marion Montgomery, *The Truth of Things: Liberal Arts and the Recovery of Reality* (Dallas: Spence, 1999).

[11]Josef Pieper, *Leisure: The Basis of Culture*, trans. Gerald Malsbary (1948; repr., South Bend, IN: St. Augustine's Press, 1998), 18.

[12]Weaver, *Visions of Order*, 118ff.

[13]Ibid., 120.

[14]Ibid.

has not lost all traces of goodness and order (sin notwith-standing). Third, whereas in gnosticism the world is to be manipulated and transformed by sinless man, in Christianity the world is to be ruled by man (Gen. 1:26ff.), even—apparently—after man's fall into sin. But this rule is meant to be under and in accord with the ultimate rulership of the triune God. Fourth, whereas gnosticism affirms that man is sinless and can do what he wants, Christianity affirms that man is sinful and must follow standards not of his own making.

The doctrine of creation also affirms that there is a thoroughgoing distinction between Creator and creature. We are simply *not* God. We receive our being from Some-one else who alone is self-existing. As creatures, we must interpret all of reality according to the God who has made us and given us life. Since the Creator God has spoken to us about the world he has created, it is *his* interpretation of reality that must pervade all of our intellectual and educa-tional endeavors. As Graeme Goldsworthy has said, "God made every fact in the universe and he alone can interpret all things and events."[15] That is, as created beings, we are not autonomous.[16] Our freedom must always be seen as a

---

[15]Graeme Goldsworthy, *According to Plan: The Unfolding Revelation of God in the Bible* (Leices-ter: Inter-Varsity, 1991), 56. This theme is particularly prominent in the writings of Cornelius Van Til. See Greg L. Bahnsen, *Van Til's Apologetic: Readings and Analysis* (Phillipsburg, NJ: P&R, 1998).

[16]When I use the word *autonomous* here, I am speaking of it in the classic liberal sense used by such thinkers as John Stuart Mill. Mill argued that the individual is the primary unit in society and that individuals own themselves. A Christian might appreciate Mill's emphasis on liberty, but a Christian's whole foundation and understanding of liberty is ultimately different. We do not own ourselves at all. We are either slaves to Christ or slaves to sin. The primary unit in society is the family (and thus neither the individual nor the omnipotent state is the primary unit). On the Christian view, then, we come into the world already in a network of relationships that render us accountable to others beside ourselves. While I cannot agree with it in all regards, the understanding of modernity and postmodernity advocated by James McClendon and Nancey Murphy is certainly helpful in thinking through these issues. See their article "Distinguishing Modern and Postmodern Theologies," *Modern Theology* 5, no. 3 (April 1989): 191–217.

THE GOSPEL AND THE MIND

created freedom, not a radical, autonomous freedom. Our learning, therefore, must always seek to understand God's interpretation of reality as revealed in Scripture, and we are always seeking to understand all of reality in light of what the triune God has spoken.[17]

Justin Martyr (ca. 100–165) is helpful when we try to construe a Christian approach to the intellectual life. Long before Nietzsche, Justin grounded our reasoning abilities in the doctrine of creation: "In the beginning He made the human race with the power of thought and of choosing the truth and of acting rightly, so that all people are without excuse before God."[18] Note that our reasoning capacity itself is rooted in being *created*, in the fact that—as created beings—we receive our being from outside of ourselves. The notion that there is a created order and thus there is a foundation for our reasoning capacities is what Nietzsche

---

[17]On this point we certainly hit an area of contention. As soon as someone speaks of "God's interpretation of reality" (which I am doing), one hears the following responses: "that is impossible"; "there is no bird's-eye view of reality"; "the Enlightenment quest for absolute certainty has failed." This position is understandable coming from the non-Christian, but when Christians begin to speak this way, it is worth stopping and taking note. I am not claiming that we can have *exhaustive* knowledge of what God thinks on this or that issue. But we can and do have *true* knowledge of what God thinks on issues. The contemporary claim (heard, if in a softer form, from some Christian thinkers) that we cannot possess any sort of metanarrative explaining and giving purpose to all of human life is at its heart a rejection of the notion that God has the ability to speak, and humans have the capacity to hear and understand such speech. Richard Lints is certainly correct that on this point Christians must reject the claim of certain "postmodern" thinkers (whatever that means) that we are so tradition bound, so embedded in our historical particularity, that we cannot have access to either transcendent truths or a metanarrative. Cf. Richard Lints, *The Fabric of Theology: A Prolegomenon to Evangelical Theology* (Grand Rapids: Eerdmans, 1993). Lints writes: "Postmodern theology has to be 'from below' because the gospel is 'from below.' The postmoderns will brook no compromise on this point—which is why there will always remain a theological chasm between the evangelical and the postmodern theological visions. The fundamental methodological movement of the evangelical theological framework is not from the ground of human experience to the superstructure of ideology but rather from the interpretive superstructure of biblical ideology to an understanding of human experience" (252). On the importance of a full-orbed doctrine of revelation, I was immensely helped early in my studies by C. S. Lewis, "Modern Theology and Biblical Criticism," in *Christian Reflections* (Grand Rapids: Eerdmans, 1967), 152–66.
[18]Justin Martyr *The First Apology* 28 (*St. Justin Martyr: The First and Second Apologies*, trans. Leslie William Barnard, Ancient Christian Writers 56 [New York: Paulist, 1997], 42).

38

opposes when he disparagingly traces the appeal to reason to a more basic appeal to creation.

We will find ourselves coming back again and again to the importance of the truth that we live in a created reality. Without a doctrine of creation, it is hard to account for the idea that there is *something there* to know. As we try to discover how the Christian vision of God, man, and the world is the necessary foundation for the intellectual life, the reality of creation will continue to assert itself.

The Centrality of History

The Christian faith takes the past seriously. At the heart of that faith is the gospel. For the Christian it is a past event that shapes the future. The death, burial, and resurrection of Jesus—a past series of events—radically shape reality now.[19] Thus, while the Christian faith has a radically future orientation, in that it looks forward to the completion of salvation and the ultimate establishment of the kingdom of God, the Christian faith also has a past orientation, in that certain first-century events—i.e., the gospel—form the axis of history and determine the trajectory of current and future events.[20]

---

[19]This reality could be illustrated by a number of Scripture references. One such example is found in Revelation 12. In the context, John speaks of a war in heaven between Michael with his angels and the dragon (v. 7). The great dragon is defeated (v. 9), and John states that Michael and his angels overcame him by the blood of the Lamb and because of the word of their testimony (v. 11). What is important to note (whether one takes Revelation 12 to be referring to first-century events, the life of the church, or some future event) is that the dragon is defeated by the blood of the Lamb (i.e., the cross), and by the word of their testimony (i.e., presumably a testimony of what Jesus had done—which would certainly include the cross and resurrection). Not only does the cross work backward (Heb. 9:15; cf. Rom. 3:25), but the power of the cross is also the means by which evil (here the dragon) in the future is defeated.

[20]For insight into the past and future components of the faith, see John Piper, *Future Grace* (Sisters, OR: Multnomah Books, 1995). *Future Grace* is more concerned with the future component of the Christian faith, although the past-looking component is not denied. Graeme Goldsworthy's work helps us to understand the centrality of the gospel for all of history. See Goldsworthy, *Gospel in Revelation: Gospel and Apocalypse* (Carlisle: Paternoster, 1994), and Goldsworthy, *According to Plan*. On the future (or eschatological) orientation of the whole

In one sense, the whole book of Deuteronomy is a lesson to the Israelites before they enter the Promised Land: Do not forget the past! Do not forget what the Lord has commanded you and what he has done for you. Even at the very end of the Old Testament, in Malachi, the last of the prophets before John and his announcement of the Messiah's coming, Scripture admonishes the Israelites to look *back*: "Remember the law of my servant Moses, the statutes and rules that I commanded him at Horeb for all Israel" (Mal. 4:4). Indeed the very last verse of Malachi speaks not simply of something new, but of a *restoration*: "He will restore the hearts of the fathers to their children . . ." (Mal. 4:6 NASB).

Biblically, the failure to remember is not always a minor oversight or inconvenience. It is often a sin. While this might sound odd to our ears, one of the chief sins of Israel was that they so often *forgot* God. For example, Deuteronomy 4:9–10 says:

> Only take care, and keep your soul diligently, lest you *forget* the things that your eyes have seen, and lest they depart from your heart all the days of your life. Make them known to your children and your children's children—how on the day that you stood before the LORD your God at Horeb, the LORD said to me, "Gather the people to me, that I may let them hear my words, so that they may learn to fear me all the days that they live on the earth, and that they may teach their children so."

A little later in Deuteronomy, Moses says:

> And if you forget the LORD your God and go after other gods and serve them and worship them, I solemnly warn you today that you shall surely perish. Like the nations that the LORD

---

of Scripture, see William J. Dumbrell, *The Search for Order: Biblical Eschatology in Focus* (Grand Rapids: Baker, 1994).

makes to perish before you, so shall you perish, because you would not obey the voice of the LORD your God. (Deut. 8:19–20)

As we will see throughout this study, the life of the mind is never really neutral. C. S. Lewis has observed that in every thought or action we are becoming either more heavenly or more hellish.[21] Our remembering (or lack thereof) "counts," in that our faithfulness (or lack thereof) is reflected by our remembering and not forgetting the Lord. See, for example, Jeremiah 2, where a sign of a decadent culture is the fact that the priests—in the midst of God's judgment on their land and culture—fail to ask a basic question, where is God?

Since the Christian faith is fundamentally *incarnational*—in that God's Son, Jesus, the second person of the Trinity, became a man in space and time—there is additional reason to emphasize the importance of history. God chose to reveal himself through a flesh-and-blood person. This person—Jesus—was born, grew up, and lived a real life with real responsibilities in a real geographical location. He got up in the morning, worked with his hands, interacted with everyday people, ate his meals, slept at night, and even grew "in wisdom and in stature and in favor with God and man" (Luke 2:52). If Jesus is the truth, and Jesus is the second person of the Trinity who lived a real historical life, then we need to reflect on what this says about the value of historical knowledge. Jesus reveals God to the world, and Jesus revealed the Father historically in time via an earthy, verifiable, flesh-and-blood life.

---

[21] This is found in Lewis, "The Weight of Glory," in *The Weight of Glory and Other Addresses* (San Francisco: HarperOne, 2001).

Torrance captures the significance of this when he points out that given the realities of the Christian faith, Christians do not come to know things merely (or primarily) through *unhistorical* knowledge. Rather, we come to know things through contact with historical realities— the life of Jesus Christ, and this life mediated to us through Holy Scripture. So writes Torrance:

> We cannot know this truth unhistorically or statically, therefore, by seeking to pass behind or beyond His action and life *in time* to what we may imagine to be the Truth in Himself, for there is no other Truth of God for us than this Truth in life and action who decisively intervenes in our human existence and pours Himself out in love to redeem us from our plight. He is not to be found or known except as He *gives* Himself to be known in space and time, that is, as He *becomes* flesh, as He *lives* His life in time and action on earth for our sake, as He *dies* upon the Cross for our salvation, and as He *rises again* from the dead for our justification. The truth of God cannot be separated from the whole historical Jesus Christ, for time, decision, action, history belong to the essential nature of this Truth. Therefore we cannot apprehend or consider the Truth in detachment from relations in space and time without downright falsification.[22]

Weaver warns that an age lacking in memory will be an age lacking in understanding: "Intelligence is this power to associate remembered potencies with things seen simply."[23] He adds, "In general all intellectuality rests upon our power to associate things not present or only suggested by what is present. Thus the intellectual value of anything depends upon our ability to retrieve from memory."[24] John Lukacs remarks similarly, "All human thinking—conscious *and*

[22]Thomas F. Torrance, *Theological Science* (London: Oxford University Press, 1969), 208–9.
[23]Weaver, *Visions of Order*, 42.
[24]Ibid., 43.

42

unconscious—depends on memory."[25] Indeed, "There is no function of the human brain that is not connected with memory."[26] Lukacs quotes Søren Kierkegaard approvingly: "We live forward, but we can only think backward."[27]

Since our age sees little value in the past, there is little emphasis on memory. And if Weaver is right, to lack memory is to lack understanding. Weaver continues, "It is therefore impossible to imagine a high-grade or effective intelligence without things supplied by the remembering process." Thus, "it seems beyond question then that any attack upon memory, insofar as this metaphor expresses real facts, is an attack upon mind."[28] Indeed, Weaver can even say, "The preservation of society is therefore directly linked with the recovery of true knowledge."[29]

If Weaver is correct on the whole, it is almost as if we are intent on destroying ourselves. By ignoring the past—the recollection of which is central to true knowledge, including knowledge of self—we are, in one sense, becoming less than fully human. And indeed, more than one twentieth-century writer commented that modern man seems to have a sort of death wish.

Malcolm Muggeridge, reflecting on his travels in the Soviet Union during the height of Stalin's planned famines (see his *Chronicles of Wasted Time*, or his novel *Winter in Moscow*[30]), spoke of his "fellow-travelers," those Western journalists, academics, union leaders, and the like, who were

---

[25]John Lukacs, *Remembered Past: John Lukacs on History, Historians, and Historical Knowledge* (Wilmington, DE: Intercollegiate Studies Institute, 2005), 764. The essay in which this remark appears, "A Student's Guide to the Study of History," was originally published by ISI under the same title in 2000.
[26]Ibid.
[27]Ibid.
[28]Weaver, *Visions of Order*, 43.
[29]Weaver, *Ideas Have Consequences*, 35.
[30]Malcolm Muggeridge, *Chronicles of Wasted Time: An Autobiography* (Washington, DC: Regnery Gateway, 1973); Muggeridge, *Winter in Moscow* (Grand Rapids: Eerdmans, 1987).

enthralled with Stalin as having a "death-wish." Weaver won-
ders whether modern man does not often seem to have a
"suicidal impulse," "or at least an impulse of self-hatred."[31]

But surely Weaver overstates his point—or does he?
He laments that modern man seems to have no memory,
no historical consciousness, no sense of identity: "No man
exists really except through that mysterious storehouse of
his remembered acts and his formed personality." Indeed,
"his very reality depends upon his carrying the past into the
present through the power of memory." Weaver concludes,
"If he does not want identity, if he has actually come to hate
himself, it is natural for him to try to get rid of memory's
baggage. He will travel light."[32]

My suggestion, then, is that the Christian faith provides
a powerful impetus for giving attention to the past, and
that without sustained attention to the past, we become—
in a very real, if morbid, sense—less than human. If Weaver
is right that human identity is wrapped up with the ability
to recollect, and if the modern age is driven by impulses
to jettison the past, then the modern age works to make
us less human. If you have ever watched a friend or loved
one suffer from Alzheimer's, this may resonate with you.
What does one say when this friend or loved one begins
to slip further and further away? We almost always say
something like, "This is not the father [or mother or friend]
I grew up with." In a sense, the inability of the person to
recollect has changed his or her identity. The person is
simply not the same person you knew, and the change
reflects a loss of personal identity rooted in the inability
to recall one's own past.

[31]Weaver, *Visions of Order*, 41.
[32]Ibid.

CREATION AND THE IMPORTANCE OF THE PAST

Memory is a part of being human, and I would suggest that attention to memory—and, more generally, the past—is inherently nurtured by historic Christianity. By emphasizing the importance of remembering God's actions, or God's revelation to us in history, the Christian faith fosters attentiveness to the past. Since the Christian faith constantly calls its adherents to attest to "the faith," "sound doctrine," "the traditions," and the like—all things that are *received*—there is likewise in the Christian faith an impetus to pay attention to what has come before. In the gospel itself we see why Christians pay attention to—and have a proper impetus for attending to—the past. The gospel is the historical reality that shapes all the rest of history. The defeat of evil in the future is ultimately tied to the gospel event itself (cf. Rev. 12:7ff.). Thus, the Christian is cognizant that a past event impinges on and shapes reality today. The Christian has every reason to attend to what has come before.

A. G. Sertillanges likewise notes the central importance of memory when he says, "We do not live by memory, we use our memory to live."[33] Pointing to the great minds of the Western intellectual tradition, Sertillanges notes, "Other things being equal, a richly filled and tenacious memory is a precious resource."[34] Likewise, "The creative faculty largely depends on the wisdom and controlled activity of the memory."[35] Sertillanges is addressing in particular the necessity of memory for the life of study. He explains, "The setting of our knowledge is the cosmos; and this is itself organization, structure. In order that the man of study may make progress it is necessary, and it suffices, that he should set up in himself, thanks to memory,

---

[33]A. G. Sertillanges, *The Intellectual Life: Its Spirit, Conditions, Methods* (Washington, DC: The Catholic University of America Press, 1998), 175.
[34]Ibid., 174.
[35]Ibid., 180.

a corresponding structure which enables him to adapt himself and thereby to act."[36]

The lack of memory, or indeed, this *attack* on memory, is widespread in our culture. It is perhaps most radically prevalent in modern academia. While the academy used to be a stronghold of love for the past—relishing old books, old languages, old truths—the contemporary academy seems to have lost its nerve in regard to the importance of the past and often seems little concerned with passing on an intellectual tradition. Perhaps the most insidious aspect of modern education is its arrogance and chronological snobbery, seen in its attempt to cut students off from the past. This war on the past is fundamentally anti-Christian in that it is essentially a gnostic obsession with the immediate. Weaver argues that such gnostics are "attackers and saboteurs of education." Indeed, "in the way they have cut the young people off from knowledge of the excellencies achieved in the past, and in the way they have turned attention toward transient externals and away from the central problem of man, they have no equal as an agency of subversion."[37] Perhaps the chief way to avoid being victim to such "attackers and saboteurs of education" is by a deep immersion in the writings of the past. Only by being saturated by the events, figures, and texts of history, can contemporary students keep from being cheated out of a good education by ideologues and educational gnostics.[38]

Christians in the academy have good biblical warrant for emphasizing the past. Christians are people who *remem-*

---

[36]Ibid., 181.
[37]Weaver, *Visions of Order*, 132–33.
[38]On this general theme, see the excellent essay by the late Mel Bradford, "Against the Barbarians," in *Against the Barbarians and Other Reflections on Familiar Themes* (Columbia, MO: University of Missouri Press, 1992), 7–16.

ber. God is not simply the God of the modern age, but the God of all of history, and if he truly has been sovereign over all of history, then history is instructive and worth studying. Since Christians view the idea of "progress" with some skepticism, they know that there is little reason to believe that all goodness and light dwells in the last one hundred years.[39] Because this is God's world, and he is sovereign, Christians recognize that the history of the world is in a sense *one* big story—the drama of creation, fall, redemption. To be educated is to know where you have come from, and this means understanding what has come before you. For Christians in the Western world, this means knowing, at least in broad terms, the flow of history, from the cradle of civilization in Mesopotamia, through the Greeks and Romans, on through the ancient, medieval, Renaissance, Reformation, and modern worlds.

Thus, any truly Christian and liberal education will be one in which students are immersed in the central texts of the past—the literature, history, philosophy, and theology of millennia. The central texts are not approached as magic talismans or as equal purveyors of wisdom. Rather, the student recognizes that the past must be approached critically (see, e.g., 2 Cor. 10:5), but also humbly, knowing that through study of such classic texts our provincial blinders are removed, captivating stories of beauty, courage, and tragedy become a part of our intellectual makeup, and we discover how our forebears dealt with numerous problems and concerns, most of which we are still wrestling with today.

The importance of history, of the past, and of learning, has been underscored by C. S. Lewis. In the fall of 1939,

---

[39]See the seminal work of Christopher Lasch, *The True and Only Heaven: Progress and Its Critics* (New York: Norton, 1991).

near the beginning of World War II, Lewis preached a sermon at University Church of St. Mary the Virgin in Oxford. "Learning in War-Time" posed a number of key questions to the Oxford students of his day, particularly: Why should you study "when the lives of our friends and the liberties of Europe are in the balance? Is it not like fiddling while Rome burns?"[40] Lewis answered the question by turning it on its head. He suggested that his own age was not necessarily unique—*all* of life is lived on "the edge of a precipice," for indeed all of life is lived against the great drama of good and evil, of persons becoming more heavenly or hellish creatures every day. In short, all of history occurs against the backdrop of heaven and hell.

Lewis went on to make some penetrating insights about the importance of history. And his point is not that of the aloof academic trying to protect his turf. Lewis was concerned for the uneducated person in the pew, who needs someone to defend him or her against the errors of the day. Indeed, Lewis argues, "Good philosophy must exist, if for no other reason, because bad philosophy needs to be answered." He continues, "The cool intellect must work not only against the cool intellect on the other side, but against the muddy heathen mysticisms which deny intellect altogether." And then he speaks to the primacy of the past:

> Most of all, perhaps, we need intimate knowledge of the past. Not that the past has any magic about it, but because we cannot study the future, and yet need something to set against the present, to remind us that the basic assumptions have been quite different in different periods and that much which seems certain to the uneducated is merely temporary fashion.

---

[40]C. S. Lewis, *The Weight of Glory and Other Addresses* (Grand Rapids: Eerdmans, 1949), 43.

There is an advantage to being grounded in history: "A man who has lived in many places is not likely to be deceived by the local errors of his native village: the scholar has lived in many times and is therefore in some degree immune from the great cataract of nonsense that pours from the press and the microphone of his own age."[41]

Given that our culture often seems unconscious of the importance of history, of the past, we must recognize that our efforts to pass on an intellectual inheritance to our children and to other children in our community will have to be more intentional than they have been. While I am not ready to head to the monastery (although it is at times tempting), Christians will have to continue to build pockets of sanity in this "perverse and wicked generation." These pockets of sanity need not have brick walls, and they should have open doors and open arms. Nonetheless Christians will surely have to be more deliberate about fostering certain habits and disciplines, with full awareness that they will receive no support from the broader culture, and at times not from the Christian church. Robert Jenson says, "If we have a calling, it is not to join a predefined intellectual enterprise *but to reinvent one*. And there is nothing preposterous about the notion, since we invented the West's intellectual enterprise in the first place."[42] In the words of Alasdair MacIntyre, at the end of his seminal work *After Virtue*, "What matters at this stage is the construction of local forms of community within which civility and the intellectual and moral life can be sustained through the new dark ages which are already upon us."[43]

---

[41]Ibid., 50–51.
[42]Robert W. Jenson, *Essays in Theology of Culture* (Grand Rapids: Eerdmans, 1995), 166.
[43]Alasdair MacIntyre, *After Virtue: A Study in Moral Theory*, 2nd ed. (Notre Dame, IN: University of Notre Dame Press, 1984), 263. C. S. Lewis's suggestion is to immerse oneself in books from the past: "Every age has its own outlook. It is specially good at seeing

Conclusion

I have suggested (1) that the Christian theological vision of the world provides the necessary theological substructure that supports the reality and importance of knowledge, learning, and the intellectual life, and (2) that without this substructure (seen here in such themes as creation and history), any meaningful intellectual life becomes tenuous, if not impossible. In short, the Christian faith affirms the reality and importance of creation and history, and without a full-orbed understanding of creation and history, any sort of meaningful intellectual life cannot be made or affirmed, at least not in a coherent manner. Without a robust understanding of creation and history, we cannot—ultimately—account for the nature of the intellectual life.

Specifically in terms of creation, I have argued the following:

1. In the Christian affirmation of a good, ordered, and governed world, we have the impetus for sustained attention to the world.

2. Because Christians affirm a created order, we are able to affirm that there is something *there* (or *here*) to be known. The world is not an illusion, but there is a created world and there is a "truth of things" to be encountered. Since there really is a world to be known, the Christian doctrine of

---

certain truths and specially liable to make certain mistakes. We all, therefore, need the books that will correct the characteristic mistakes of our own period." Further: "The only palliative is to keep the clean sea breeze of the centuries blowing through our minds, and this can be done only by reading old books. Not, of course, that there is any magic about the past. People were no cleverer then than they are now; they made as many mistakes as we. But not the *same* mistakes . . . . To be sure, the books of the future would be just as good a corrective as the books of the past, but unfortunately we cannot get at them." C. S. Lewis, "Introduction" to Athanasius, *On the Incarnation* (Crestwood, NY: St. Vladimir's Seminary Press, 2000), 4–5. This essay can also be found in Lewis, "On the Reading of Old Books," in *God in the Dock: Essays in Theology and Ethics*, ed. Walter Hooper (Grand Rapids: Eerdmans, 1973), 200–207.

creation encourages, and ultimately provides the necessary precondition for, a meaningful intellectual life.

Also, for a number of reasons the Christian faith sustains and encourages attention to the past, hence the importance of history:

1. The gospel—as a past-tense event that is the apex of history and is still active in the world today—points Christians to the importance of looking *back* for wisdom, insight, and understanding in the present.

2. Similarly, since Christians are not gnostics and believe that revelation is mediated—through both word and deed—we again have reason to pay attention to what has come before. Given the nature of the Christian faith, we have reason to look back, and we have an impetus to *receive*, and this reception of revelation comes through particular acts in history, and through particular texts—Holy Writ (itself the product of a tradition passed on).

3. Given that the people of God in both the Old and New Testaments are accountable for what God has spoken, Christians put a premium on remembering, and this, again, is an impetus for giving attention to what has come before. So there is a moral accountability for what has been given us, and we should be a people of memory. One thinks of the Passover meal (Exodus 12–13) and of Jesus' instruction to take the Lord's Supper "in *remembrance* of me" (Luke 22:19). In an age that does not place a high premium on the past (likely a result of unbelief), Christians must see themselves as countercultural in their emphasis on memory and must be particularly diligent to cultivate and practice the habit of remembering. Remembering is—ultimately—a virtue. And given that our culture discourages this particular virtue, Christians must find ways of intentionally cultivating this practice.

As Christians attempt both to strengthen the church and to evangelize the lost, it will be essential to embody viable and vibrant communities where the intellectual life and learning can occur to the glory of God. Why should our children feel compelled to become immersed in an ancient tradition called the Christian faith when our culture—and often the church—by its actions shows little reverence for the past? In C. S. Lewis's words, speaking of how modern culture, modern education in particular, shapes young boys and girls without virtue or heart: "In a sort of ghastly simplicity we remove the organ and demand the function. We make men without chests and expect of them virtue and enterprise. We laugh at honour and are shocked to find traitors in our midst. We castrate and bid the geldings be fruitful."[44] The recovery of a meaningful and sustainable intellectual life will most fully take place only within traditions rooted in the gospel, and where a gospel-driven and gospel-supported appreciation for the centrality of creation and the past are given their proper place.

---

[44]C. S. Lewis, *The Abolition of Man* (New York: Simon and Schuster, 1944), 37.

Now all rational thinking in all the sciences, following the way of analysis, terminates in the knowledge of divine science.

THOMAS AQUINAS

What do they not see, who look upon Him, Who sees all?

GREGORY THE GREAT

We have abundant scientific knowledge of our world and technical mastery over it. But its meaning is hidden from us. We have knowledge of the facts, and knowledge of the means, but no knowledge of the end.

ROGER SCRUTON

From Aristotle to Aquinas and beyond, any motion is invested with purpose . . . . The world itself is suffused with purposefulness, with a goal, or an "end." And every person's life must be understood in terms of its purpose.

A. J. CONYERS III

2

The Centrality of a Telos
to All Things

It is common in the academy these days to speak of
"modernity" and "postmodernity" (or related words). Any
young graduate student trying to make his or her way
through virtually any field of study will have to navigate
waters filled with questions related to defining or understanding or explaining the nature of the so-called modern
and postmodern worlds. Indeed, virtually all of one's studies
can be absorbed in just these issues. And ultimately, such
questions are worthy of study. Throughout history man has
plotted his way in the world, attempted to understand his
place in history, and sought to identify what is unique about
his day, what distinguishes his own time from other eras.
Often certain narratives become dominant, taking on a life
of their own as *the* way to understand one's own times.

Unfortunately, such dominant explanations can become impervious to criticism. They simply become a given, and any questioning of such paradigms or narratives becomes verboten.

One current narrative attempting to explain the nature and origin of modernity goes something like this: In the 1600s, the European continent had experienced decades of civil wars, all tied to religious rivalries and claims. In light of the apparent failure of religion to provide sound roots for civil society, René Descartes arose in a quest for certainty. Unlike those who had preceded him, Descartes sought *absolute* certainty, and thus set out to find some neutral and universal (i.e., nonreligious) foundation for his own intellectual program. Descartes believed he had found his indubitable foundation in the thinking and doubting self, hence his maxim *cogito ergo sum* ("I think, therefore I am"). Inasmuch as Descartes sought to build his system with the solitary, autonomous, reasoning man at the center, he is one of the founders of modern thought and a forerunner of the full-blown Enlightenment that would come with thinkers like David Hume and Immanuel Kant.[1]

---

[1]This basic narrative is found in numerous places. For one among many, see Stephen Toulmin, *Cosmopolis* (Chicago: University of Chicago Press, 1990). Toulmin offers a nice summary of the view above (80–81), although his own view is somewhat different. There are certainly other views. Colin Gunton seeks to root much of modernity in impulses that were exacerbated in the Western tradition by Augustine. Richard Weaver sees the problems of modernity as most naturally rooted in the thought of William of Occam and the victory of nominalism. On Gunton, see, among other things, his *The One, the Three and the Many: God, Creation and the Culture of Modernity*, The Bampton Lectures 1992 (Cambridge: Cambridge University Press, 1994). For a critique of Gunton, see Brad Green, "The Protomodern Augustine? Colin Gunton and the Failure of Augustine," *International Journal of Systematic Theology* 9, no. 3 (2007): 328–41. This essay is a distillation of my longer work, *Colin Gunton and the Failure of Augustine: The Theology of Colin Gunton in Light of Augustine* (Eugene, OR: Wipf and Stock, 2010). On Weaver, see *Ideas Have Consequences* (Chicago: University of Chicago Press, 1948). More recently, see Thomas Fleming, *Morality in Everyday Life: Rediscovering an Ancient Alternative to the Liberal Tradition* (Columbia, MO: University of Missouri Press, 2004). One of the most fascinating accounts of modernity in recent years is John Milbank, *Theology and Social Theory: Beyond Secular Reason*, 2nd ed. (London: Wiley-Blackwell, 2006).

At this point in the narrative, there are some options. One popular version, in attempting to understand Christianity's place in the story, goes like this: Christians responded to this intellectual current in a number of ways. The more conservative stream of Christianity generally bought into the basic premises of the Enlightenment— the quest/need for certainty, autonomous individualism, the centrality of reason—and from that vantage point tried to articulate a Christian response to the Enlightenment. This effort was doomed to fail, for these Christians naively assumed the very presuppositions and worldview to which they should have been offering a constructive and biblical alternative.[2] Thus, as some see it, this more conservative stream of Christianity did not really respond to the Enlightenment, but rather was already co-opted by Enlightenment thinking.

As the narrative continues, the more usual suspects receive attention—Hobbes, Locke, and others. And there is much that is insightful in this narrative. The question of certainty, the reality of autonomous individualism, and the rise of rationalism are all part of the picture. But the premodern world, particularly in its Christian form, was animated—at least in part—by another reality, and the eclipse of this reality in the modern world goes a long way toward illustrating the differences between the contemporary and the premodern worlds. In short, while the premodern—and generally Christian—world was animated by a sense of a telos (a goal) toward which all things are heading, the modern

---

[2]Some then argue that in the quest for certainty, conservative Christians were trying to meet the Enlightenment's demand for absolute certainty by making the case for an inerrant Bible, and in part succeeded. Thus, for example, goes the narrative as seen in the recent works of John Franke and the late Stanley Grenz. See especially Stanley J. Grenz and John R. Franke, *Beyond Foundationalism: Shaping Theology in a Postmodern Context* (Louisville, KY: Westminster John Knox, 2001). See, more recently, Franke, *Manifold Witness: The Plurality of Truth* (Nashville: Abingdon, 2009).

world generally lacked a grand and transcendent telos. In A. J. Conyers's words, the modern world was marked by a tragic "eclipse of heaven."[3]

In this chapter I want to explore this notion of an eclipse of heaven or, put differently, the loss of a sense of a telos or goal animating and structuring reality and history, and providing the backdrop for the intellectual life. It is impossible to fully summarize the history of any era briefly, but it is safe to say that one key element of modernity has been its abandonment of any sense of a transcendent telos that informs life in the here and now. The history of modern thought, on the whole, is a history of skepticism, misplaced optimism, and intellectual dead ends. Among other things, it has been one long story, to quote G. K. Chesterton, of "reason in the void."[4]

The question that informs this entire book—what is the link between the gospel and the intellectual life?—raises another question worthy of attention: If the Christian gospel is the central event in history, and therefore if the death, burial, and resurrection of Jesus lie at the heart of all meaning, then is there any link between the wanderings and degeneration of modern thought and the loss of the Christian gospel as the central integrating reality? When Mark Noll wrote *The Scandal of the Evangelical Mind*, he suggested that the "scandal" in question was that there *was no* evangelical mind, bright spots notwithstanding.[5] But that is only half the question. The more pressing question might be, What does the gospel have to do with the retrieval and cultivation of any meaningful intellec-

---

[3]A. J. Conyers, *The Eclipse of Heaven: Rediscovering the Hope of a World Beyond* (Downers Grove, IL: InterVarsity, 1992).
[4]G. K. Chesterton, *Orthodoxy* (San Francisco: Ignatius, 1995), 32, writes that one of the marks of insanity is "reason used without root, reason in the void."
[5]Mark Noll, *The Scandal of the Evangelical Mind* (Grand Rapids: Eerdmans, 1994).

tual life whatsoever? In other chapters of this book I deal explicitly with creation, the cross, language, and the moral nature of knowledge. In this chapter I want to ask what the future, or in more theological terms, eschatology—here in the sense of a telos or goal in history—has to do with the cultivation of a meaningful intellectual life.

I've suggested that, whereas much of modern thought appears to be adrift with no direction or purpose, pre-modern Christian thinkers almost always engaged in intellectual endeavors against the backdrop of an overarching telos or goal. With Augustine and the medieval tradition that followed him, the telos of the vision of God was the goal that animated and informed his intellectual deliberations. This goal could be stated in different ways. Like Augustine, Thomas and Dante spoke of the vision of God as the ultimate telos of man. Man is on a journey to the city of God, and the climax of this journey is to one day see God face-to-face. This journey motif informs much of the Western intellectual tradition, whether in Chaucer's *Canterbury Tales*, Bunyan's *Pilgrim's Progress*, or even Tolkien's *The Hobbit* and *Lord of the Rings* trilogy. Even when the common Christian was not meditating on what this vision of God might be like (as Augustine was doing in *The Trinity*), the notion that we are all pilgrims on a journey to the city of God was the default mode of thinking, the cultural consensus for the Christian West. And when this larger telos was lost, much else was lost besides.[6]

For example, in speaking of modernity, A. J. Conyers suggests that motion becomes a central theme, but a motion without any end or goal in sight. As Conyers has written:

---

[6]Cf. the excellent essay by David Lyle Jeffrey, "Masterplot and Meaning in the Biblical Narrative," *Houses of the Interpreter: Reading Scripture, Reading Culture* (Waco, TX: Baylor University Press, 2003), 15–38.

> What drops out of the picture [with modernity] along with the beginning of motion, however, is also the "end" of motion—in other words the "goal" or the purpose of motion. From Aristotle to Aquinas and beyond, any motion is invested with purpose. . . . The world itself is suffused with purposefulness, with a goal, or an "end." And every person's life must be understood in terms of its purpose.[7]

Instead of seeing motion as *headed somewhere*, modern thinkers came to see motion as simply motion, with no particular goal or end in sight.

Conversely, Josef Pieper, writing about how human freedom is realized in the knowing process, says this:

> Whenever someone contemplates reality in pure pursuit of knowledge and without regard for immediate practical purposes; whenever someone, oblivious of possible usefulness, disadvantages, danger, or even death, is able to say, "So it is; this is the truth" (e.g., "The Emperor has no clothes!")—then we witness, in an eminent degree, human freedom in action.[8]

Pieper is arguing that man's achievement of his ultimate end requires some kind of existence beyond this temporal, earth-bound realm.[9]

The telos of the beatific vision of God—the thought of seeing him face-to-face one day—impressed upon premodern Christians that the intellectual life is not simply its own end but contributes to a larger goal, the glory of God. While the notion of a telos or goal is not *distinctively* Christian, it

---

[7]A. J. Conyers, *The Listening Heart: Vocation and the Crisis of Modern Culture* (Dallas: Spence, 2006), 155. This was Conyers's last work before his premature death, and I believe it was his best. Readers wanting a penetrating analysis of the nature of modernity would do well to find this volume.
[8]Josef Pieper, *Abuse of Language, Abuse of Power*, trans. Lothar Krauth (1974; repr., San Francisco: Ignatius, 1988), 49.
[9]Ibid.

certainly took root in the Christian soil of the West as the gospel spread throughout the world.

But the notion of a telos is certainly not confined to the Jewish-Christian tradition. Aristotle, among many others, spoke of a telos to the nature of things in general, and to the nature of human life in particular. And two recent efforts to justify the intellectual life in terms of a telos, yet *not* on Christian grounds, are the works of Roger Scruton and Allan Bloom. Both Scruton and Bloom are something of iconoclasts in that they resist the acidic skepticism and nihilism of the contemporary intellectual milieu. They both are traditionalists of sorts in that they believe in the possibility of meaning, the reality of truth, and the necessity of actually teaching central texts and engaging in meaningful conversations about what Russell Kirk called the "permanent things."

The Notion of Teleology in Contemporary Secular Thought

Scruton and Bloom are two illustrations that there is something about the notion of a telos or goal to human existence that is hard for contemporary persons to shake. The idea that history is heading somewhere is part and parcel of a Christian understanding of reality: there really is a God who has created the world; the world has fallen into sin; and this good God is now governing, ruling, and directing all of reality to its appointed end. Thus there is a trajectory that informs and helps constitute all of reality. This is not to say that Christians pretend they can detect in some exhaustive sense all traces of this trajectory. But Christians nonetheless affirm the existence of this goal as part of the world in which we live.

Steve Fuller of the University of Warwick is among the many who have argued that it is the Christian vision of reality—particularly in its Protestant form—that was at the heart of the origin of modern science.[10] Fuller suggests that what Alister McGrath calls "Christianity's dangerous idea"— that people can read and study the Bible and actually come to know something true of the God of the universe—was central to the birth of modern science. When attention to the created order was combined with attention to Holy Writ, it drove certain persons to ask fundamental questions about the nature of reality. They were thus led to engage in scientific discovery, scientific inquiry, and scientific deliberation.

Yet Roger Scruton and Allan Bloom are among many contemporary thinkers who, though not explicitly Christian, utilize a notion of telos or goal in their writings. We cannot explore all of the reasons why secular thought may parallel that of Christians. But if we are created beings who are hard wired to serve and worship and know the triune Creator of the universe, it makes sense that even the non-Christian has an "echo" or "memory" of eternity. Though non-Christians do not bow the knee to the risen Jesus, they "know" God (see Rom. 1:19, 21) and engage in intellectual deliberations in reliance on—and indebtedness to—a Christian vision of God, man, and the world. Let's look more closely at the examples of Scruton and Bloom.

Roger Scruton

Roger Scruton, an English philosopher (b. 1944), like many other contemporary thinkers, appears at times to glimpse

---

[10]Steve Fuller, *Dissent Over Descent: Intelligent Design's Challenge to Darwinism* (London: Icon, 2008). See also Fuller's chapter, in *Should Christians Embrace Evolution? Biblical and Scientific Responses*, ed. Norman C. Nevin (Nottingham: Inter-Varsity, 2010).

the Christian vision of things, at least a shadowy form of the Christian vision. In the conclusion to his book, *An Intelligent Person's Guide to Modern Culture*, Scruton laments the loss of meaning in modern culture:

> We have abundant scientific knowledge of our world and technical mastery over it. But its meaning is hidden from us. We have knowledge of the facts, and knowledge of the means, but no knowledge of the end. My purpose in this book has been to illustrate this peculiar ignorance—not ignorance *that*, or ignorance *how* but ignorance *what*. We no longer know what to do or what to feel; the meaninglessness of our world is a projection of our numbness towards it.[11]

Where does Scruton turn to answer the *what* questions: To what end are we living our lives? To what end are we studying? To what end are we learning? One might expect him to turn to some transcendent source of meaning. Instead Scruton turns to "culture." "Culture supplies what is missing—the knowledge [of] what to feel which comes with the invocation of our true community. . . . And that is the point of high culture: neither to 'do dirt on life,' nor to emphasise its senselessness, but to recuperate by imaginative means the old experience at home."[12] Like so many critics of modernity, Scruton borrows various Christian themes or insights, even if these are not always gathered up as a coherent whole. He even gives evidence of a kind of eschatological hope and even uses Christian historical imagery to illustrate his point:

> But here and there, sheltered from the noise and glare of the media, the old spiritual forces are at work. . . . To those who wish

---

[11] Roger Scruton, *The Intelligent Person's Guide to Modern Culture* (South Bend, IN: St. Augustine's Press, 2000), 155.
[12] Ibid.

for it, the ethical life may still be retrieved. Ours is a catacomb culture, a flame kept alive by undaunted monks. And what the monks of Europe achieved in a former dark age, they might achieve again.[13]

Ultimately, however, rather than turning to Saint Benedict (480–547)—a monk of monks!—Scruton turns to Confucius.[14] Yet, even in giving the nod to Confucius, Scruton is "recommending" him only because attention to Confucius allows us to live life *as if* we live in a divinely created and governed world:

> Confucius did not offer any metaphysical system or religious creed. Instead he enjoined us to live *as if* it matters eternally what we do: to obey the rites, the ceremonies and the customs that lend dignity to our actions and which lift them above the natural sphere; to cultivate the heart and tongue so that beauty is always in and around us; and to live in the condition which Wordsworth called "natural piety," acknowledging the greatness of creation, and the imponderable mystery of our time. In this way *even if we have no religious beliefs*, we acknowledge the existence of sacred things, and endow our gestures with a nimbus of the supernatural. *Living thus we peer serenely into the eternal.*[15]

Provocatively, Scruton ends his book with the lines, "Confucius did not give us faith; but he gives us hope."[16] Scruton's goal of meaning, morality, a sense of human dignity, and purpose all seem to cry out for the reality of the divine. But—sadly—the best Scruton can offer is an appeal to Confucius, perhaps in an attempt to salvage the benefits

[13]Ibid., 156.
[14]Saint Benedict is considered the founder of Western monasticism and is often regarded as a key figure who helped Christianity weather the so-called Dark Ages.
[15]Scruton, *The Intelligent Person's Guide to Modern Culture*, 158. Emphasis mine.
[16]Ibid.

of living as if the divine exists without having to embrace the reality.

Allan Bloom

We find something similar in Allan Bloom. His 1987 work, *The Closing of the American Mind,* has become something of a classic.[17] Its publication ignited a discussion about the nature of higher education in North America and garnered both high praise and intense criticism along generally predictable lines—conservatives tended to like it, liberals did not.

For our purposes it is worth noting that Bloom—like virtually anyone who is serious about the life of the mind—affirms a type of telos as central to education. For example, "The teacher, particularly the teacher dedicated to liberal education, must constantly try to look toward the goal of human completeness. . . ."[18] Similarly, "What each generation is can be best discovered in its relation to the permanent concerns of mankind."[19] Bloom adds:

> No real teacher can doubt that his task is to assist his pupil to fulfill human nature against all the deforming forces of convention and prejudice. The vision of what that nature is may be clouded, the teacher may be more or less limited, but his activity is solicited by something beyond him that at the same time provides him with a standard for judging his students' capacity and achievement.[20]

Bloom wishes to affirm one of the central ideals of classical education—the goal of education is to produce a certain

---

[17]Allan Bloom, *The Closing of the American Mind: How Higher Education Has Failed Democracy and Impoverished the Souls of Today's Students* (New York: Simon and Schuster, 1987).
[18]Ibid., 19.
[19]Ibid.
[20]Ibid., 20.

kind of person: "Every educational system has a moral goal that it tries to attain and that informs its curriculum. It wants to produce a certain kind of human being."[21] This implies an anthropology at work in Bloom's thinking about education. He is convinced "that there is a human nature, and that assisting its fulfillment is his [the teacher's] task."[22]

But if Bloom recognizes and affirms the centrality of a telos, it is a telos construed mainly along non-Christian classical lines, the formation of the philosopher king. Now, certainly a Christian could conceivably construe this goal along Christian lines, but this is not what Bloom is doing. Still, Bloom's critique is worth hearing. Bloom laments that higher education in the United States has abandoned its mission of forming wise men and women, and has deserted the traditional high calling of passing on an intellectual tradition, and of grounding students in such a tradition. This is indeed a sad state of affairs and worthy of attention. In response, Bloom gravitates toward religion as a virtual precondition of meaningful culture and intellectual life. He writes: "A life based on the Book is closer to the truth, . . . it provides the material for deeper research in and access to the nature of things. Without the great revelations, epics and philosophies as part of our natural vision, there is nothing to see out there, and eventually little left inside."[23]

Bloom makes clear that he is not calling for the centrality of the gospel, and yet he cannot avoid bumping into religion as virtually essential to the cultured, educated life. As Scruton turns to Confucius, Bloom turns to the classical notion of the ideal man, filtered through enlightenment notions of democracy and equality. We do not find here a call for a

---

[21] Ibid., 26.
[22] Ibid., 19.
[23] Ibid., 60.

full-orbed, Christ-centered, intellectual life. We do find a telos and something of a proposed solution, but we do not see a call to the ultimate ground of truth.

Christians can share in the lament that the older curriculum has been discarded. But neither thinker grounds his intellectual deliberations in an explicitly Christian understanding of the nature of things. Both are—in one sense—heirs of the Enlightenment. Christians cannot be satisfied with the Enlightenment as the ground on which to recover the intellectual life. We have to go back further to when the life of the mind was seen in relationship to— and as a constituent part of—a larger vision of God, man, and the world. All of life is lived in a pilgrimage to the city of God. Whether someone recognizes this pilgrimage is another question, but on Christian terms, all of life should be lived in light of one's ultimate destiny. To return to the Enlightenment is not the solution but merely an intensification of the problem.

Back to the Beginning

Ultimately, the notion of a telos or goal that informs all of human life finds its most significant theological rootage in the Bible and, flowing from that, the Christian intellectual tradition. For example, in Genesis 2, God placed the man in the garden and gave him a purpose. He was "to cultivate ['abad] it and keep [samar] it" (Gen. 2:15 NASB). Here "to cultivate" denotes that man is to do something with creation, while "keep" appears to denote that there is something in this aspect of the created order worth preserving. In other words, God did not place man in the garden simply to sip lattes and enjoy the beauty of his surroundings. There is something worth preserving, and there is also work to be done. History is going somewhere.

As William Dumbrell has argued in his book *The Search for Order: Biblical Eschatology in Focus*, the eschatological focus of the Bible is concerned not simply with this or that end-times scheme, but with the pervasive and overarching eschatological structure of the Bible as a whole, including just such passages as Genesis 2:15.[24] One of the key theses of this book is that when such an eschatological focus begins to lose hold in a culture, we should expect to see a lack of a meaningful intellectual and cultural life. Experience in the here and now—including the intellectual life—becomes fragmented and disordered once ripped out of a larger and more beautiful and more life-giving vision of things.

The Liberal Arts

To uncover the premodern understanding of purposeful history and culture, it is helpful to look at the notion of the *artes liberals*, or the liberal arts. In the contemporary academy, the liberal arts have often been either effectively abandoned—even if the term *liberal arts* continues to be used in a generally positive way within a particular institution—or more explicitly rejected in favor of professional or technical training. A third option, often advocated by more traditional colleges, including some Christian colleges, speaks of the liberal arts as those courses which make up a "core curriculum" or the study of "Great Books," or as that sequence of courses which can help form a "well-rounded person." This understanding of the liberal arts is not really bad, though it is incomplete.

The *liberal* arts, as they were developed in the Christian West, were construed in contrast to the *servile* arts. The

---

[24]William J. Dumbrell, *The Search for Order: Biblical Eschatology in Focus* (Grand Rapids: Baker, 1994).

former were "liberal" in that they were the arts of the free person (the Latin *libera* means "free"). "Free" in this sense denoted persons with the leisure time to contemplate the eternal verities. The servile arts, on the other hand, were the skills of "unfree" persons, those engaged in commerce, business, or a trade, who had to get their hands dirty in the day-to-day tasks of making deals, politicking, and so forth (*servile* comes from the Latin word meaning "slave" or "servant"). Thus, the liberal arts were *not* primarily skills or techniques that could be pressed into immediate service in the marketplace or used to advance oneself quickly in the world of commerce. The liberal arts were intentionally useless.[25] They were not first and foremost utilitarian.

In the temporal realm, the liberal arts were seen as a way of forming a certain kind of person. Both Christians and non-Christians saw the liberal arts as a means of forming wise and virtuous people. In the eternal or heavenly realm, Christians believed that the liberal arts indeed had an eternal purpose. These arts were a way of training the mind so that one could contemplate God in eternity. Thus, a school was a place of "leisure." As Pieper explains in his book *Leisure: The Basis of Culture*, originally published in 1948, the *school* was indeed a place where one should— for a time—be "useless" in the sense of practicing the art of leisure, rest, and contemplation.[26] As Pieper notes, the Latin term *schola*, from which we get our word *school*, actually means "leisure" or "rest." While work is a creation ordinance, and it is fundamentally a good thing, it does not appear to be an *ultimate* thing. The liberal arts, however,

---

[25]For a short treatment, see Peter J. Leithart, "For Useless Learning," *First Things*, November 2000, 11–12.
[26]Josef Pieper, *Leisure: The Basis of Culture*, trans. Gerald Malsbary (1948; repr., South Bend, IN: St. Augustine's Press, 1998).

were a way of preparing for our ultimate rest—the eternal contemplation and vision of God.

What are the implications of all this? Simply this: that in the premodern and Christian way of viewing the intellectual life, education or learning had that ultimate goal in mind. Christians explicitly understood and construed the intellectual life in eschatological and heavenly terms. This is not to say that the intellectual endeavor was only preparatory, or that there was no purpose here and now for the intellectual life. Both the *trivium* ("verbal" arts—grammar, logic, and rhetoric) and the *quadrivium* ("mathematical" arts—geometry, arithmetic, music, astronomy) were meant to form a certain type of person—wise, virtuous, and eloquent. Even in the temporal realm this person reflected upon—and was marked by attention to—truth, goodness, and beauty. But at the very same time, this person was being prepared for his or her ultimate destiny—the vision and contemplation of God.[27] And once this telos was lost—the goal of becoming a certain kind of person, of one day seeing God face-to-face, of being a part of some larger and transcendent goal in history—then lost with it were the *reasons* for doing things that have meaning only in relationship to that larger telos.

Athanasius and the Way Things Ought to Be
When reading premodern texts, one is often struck by terms, ideas, tendencies, and mindsets that repeatedly assert themselves. When I first read Athanasius's *On the Incarnation* all the way through, I knew that he was a hero of the faith and that he had done much to forge and articulate Nicene

---

[27]The liberal arts have gone through various permutations. See D. G. Hart, "Education and Alienation: What John Henry Newman Could Learn from Wendell Berry," *Touchstone*, October 2005, 31–35.

orthodoxy. But I was impressed by something more than his polemical prowess, a turn of phrase, or a stunning argument. Rather, I was captivated by how he *thought* theologically.

An example is his explanation of why the Word became flesh, why the second person of the Trinity became incarnate. Athanasius argues that because of sin, the created order had become corrupted, and without the incarnation this corruption would continue until there was ultimately nothing left (or at least nothing *good* left) of the created order. And this, Athanasius argues, would simply be "unfitting."[28] He continues, "It would, of course, have been unthinkable that God should go back upon His word and that man, having transgressed, should not die; but it was equally monstrous that beings which once had shared the nature of the Word should perish and turn back again into nonexistence through corruption."[29]

This reasoning originally struck me as odd. *Unfitting?* But Athanasius makes this kind of argument repeatedly. And even if one would not defend the incarnation on that particular ground (i.e., the *fittingness* of the notion that God would intervene to rescue the created order), it is worth asking *why* Athanasius argues this way.

Athanasius can turn to fittingness because he believes certain things about God and creation and how the two relate. Athanasius can appeal to the way things *ought* to be because there is apparently broad enough agreement among his audience. Note that Athanasius does not simply engage in proof-texting. Rather, he makes an argument that moves from (1) the fittingness of creation to (2) the need of redemption to (3) the incarnation. Though Athanasius

---

[28]This way of thinking runs throughout *On the Incarnation*. For example, in 2.6 it would be "unworthy" of God, and "unfitting" that God should allow his good creation to "turn back again into non-existence," or to "be brought to nothing."
[29]Ibid.

does indeed make appeals to Scripture, he and his audience apparently share an understanding of the way things ought to be. And this affirmation of what ought to be is ultimately an eschatological vision that informs and drives his intellectual deliberations, leading to other theological assertions and arguments. His telos—the way things *ought* to be—drives his case for the incarnation.

Augustine and the Eschatological Vision
Augustine provides one of the best examples of Christian intellectual deliberation. Like many premodern Christian writers, Augustine was a bishop, or pastor, and his writings are thus informed by the existential and pastoral questions of his day. Whether meeting the challenge of Pelagianism from inside the confessing church or refuting pagan detractors of Christianity who blamed the Christian faith for the downfall of Rome (see *The City of God*), most of what Augustine wrote emerged out of pastoral issues he himself encountered.

My interest here is in the way Augustine theologizes, particularly in his classic work *The Trinity*, often recognized as a seminal work on that crucial doctrine. *The Trinity* is helpful in illustrating what made the premodern Christian mind tick. Augustine makes clear that he believes in the Trinity on the basis of Scripture and tradition. He is happy to "receive" this doctrine in the best sense. Why then does he add to the tradition hundreds of pages on the doctrine? As Edmund Hill explains, Augustine is engaging in a type of *via inventionis*—a way of discovery—which is different from Thomas's *Summa theologiae*, which is more of a *via doctrinae*—a way of doctrine. When reading *The Trinity*, one gets the sense that Augustine is exploring what this received doctrine means, and he is allowing the reader to peer over his shoulder as he discovers what the Trinity is. Augustine is quite happy to entertain an analogy or follow a train of thought, only to discard it when he decides that line of reasoning is unfruitful.

But more is going on here than simply playing with ideas, and this is key to our discussion here. Augustine has a larger and grander motivation for his theologizing. The text that serves as a type of theological backbone to the work is 1 Corinthians 13:12, "For now we see in a mirror dimly, but then face to face. Now I know in part; then I shall know fully, even as I have been fully known." Augustine turns to this verse repeatedly. Why? Because he believes that one day he will see God in person, and he is thus concerned to ask, what is this God like whom I will see face-to-face? A larger theological and eschatological vision of life informs Augustine's exploration of the Trinity. Augustine believes he is going to meet God and look into his face, and this ultimate destiny then informs and inspires his theological deliberations as to what God is like.

Augustine writes in his *Soliloquies* that faith, hope, and love are necessary for a person to truly know or see God. He adds,

> The attentive view is now followed by the very vision of God, which is the end of looking; not because the power of beholding ceases, but because it has nothing further to which it can turn itself: and this is the truly perfect virtue, virtue arriving at its end, which is followed by the life of blessedness.[30]

---

[30]Augustine *Soliloquies* 1.13 (*Nicene and Post-Nicene Fathers*, Series 1, 7:541). A half century earlier Athanasius wrote, toward the end of *On the Incarnation* (9.57): "But for the searching and right understanding of the Scriptures there is need of a good life and a pure soul, and for Christian virtue to guide the mind to grasp, so far as human nature can, the truth concerning God the Word. One cannot possibly understand the teaching of the saints unless one has a pure mind and is trying to imitate their life." Hugh of St. Victor (d. 1141) wrote (approvingly in reference to Socrates) that "the eye of the heart must be cleansed by the study of virtue, so that it may thereafter see clearly for the investigation of truth in the theoretical arts." See

Why is this so significant? It is further evidence that at the heart of the Christian premodern understanding of theology, if not the more general understanding of the intellectual life as well, was the eschatological vision of God. Rather than the goal of theology simply being to "get it right," or "to develop a perfect system," premodern Christian thought, at least as exemplified by Augustine, was concerned to theologize against the backdrop of that eschatological and relational reality. Only when this ultimate purpose of human existence is understood—this anticipation of seeing the face of God that animates Augustine's theologizing—can we appreciate the logic of Augustine's *De Trinitate*.

Interestingly, Augustine spends two books (4 and 13) largely on the atoning work of Christ, when he is supposed to be writing on the Trinity.[31] Is this an anomaly? I would argue not. While Augustine holds out to us the fulfillment of 1 Corinthians 13:12—of one day seeing God face-to-face—to reach such a vision we must be purified

Hugh of St. Victor, *Didascalicon*, trans. Jerome Taylor (New York: Columbia University Press, 1991), 154. I reference Athanasius and Hugh of St. Victor to point out that on a Christian understanding of the intellectual life, knowledge of God requires that the knower has been spiritually transformed. Augustine can speak explicitly of having a mind purified by the cross, and Athanasius and Hugh are both in the same world when they speak of a "good life and a pure soul" (Athanasius) or say that "the eye of the heart must be cleansed" (Hugh).

[31] In Augustine scholarship there is a debate on whether *The Trinity* is an irenic and exploratory work or a polemical work. I treat this in *Colin Gunton and the Failure of Augustine*. Cf. George Lawless, *Augustine: Presbyter Factus Sum*, Collectanea Augustiniana (New York: Peter Lang, 1993), 7; Roland Kany, "'Fidei Contemnentes Initium': On Certain Positions Opposed by Augustine in *The Trinity*," ed. Elizabeth A. Livingstone, Studia Patristica 27 (Leuven: Peeters, 1993), 327. Opinions vary regarding Augustine's opponents and his ultimate purposes in *The Trinity*. See Michel René Barnes, "The Arians of Book V, and the Genre of *De Trinitate*," *Journal of Theological Studies*, ns, 44, no. 1 (1993): 185–95; Barnes, "Exegesis and Polemic in Augustine's *De Trinitate* I," *Augustinian Studies* 30 (1999): 43–59. Much of Augustine scholarship sees Augustine's christological opponents in the Eunomians. Barnes is arguing against the weight of this view among the following scholars: Michael Schmaus, *Die psychologische Trinitätslehre des heilegen Augustinus* (Münster: Aschendorffsche Verlagsbuchhandlung, 1927), 143; Alfred Schindler, *Wort und Analogie in Augustine Trinitätslehre* (Tübingen: Mohr, 1965), 151–53; Olivier du Roy, *L'intelligence de la foi en la Trinité selon saint Augustin* (Paris: Études Augustiniennes, 1966), 458.

and transformed. And Augustine argues that the path to such a vision travels through the cross. In short, whereas the Neoplatonist argued that one could reach God (or "the One") via human effort, Augustine contends that in order for man to progress up to God, God had to first come down to us in the form of a man, and had to sacrifice himself on the cross. Only through this sacrifice can we be "fitted" for heaven.[32]

What do we learn from this glance at Augustine? Fundamentally that, like many before him, Augustine thinks in terms of a telos, the vision of God, that then informs his theologizing. This conviction then shapes the way he thinks about the Trinity, the incarnation, and the cross. He, in a sense, works *backward* from the telos of the vision of God as he explores and articulates other theological convictions and beliefs.

Perhaps because we have grown up in and have been conditioned by a culture that does not see the inherent unity of all things, we have a tendency to view the intellectual life (even cognition itself) as a neutral or autonomous realm. In so many dimensions of our lives, we are probably functional atheists, in that we do not even begin to see how the lordship of the risen Jesus relates to our understanding, learning, or thinking. But if the Christian story is the one true narrative—and such a conviction is simply the inheritance of Christianity itself, though more forcefully and impressively articulated by such persons as N. T. Wright and John Milbank in recent years—then indeed

---

[32]It is unfortunate that some hymn editors have felt compelled to disregard the notion of being "fitted" for heaven. The older version of "Away in a Manger" contained the words "and fit us for heaven," while some more modern versions replace this with "and *take* us to heaven." The difference may seem negligible, but it is worth noting. Being "fit" for heaven denotes that we must be transformed and changed if we are going to enter into the presence of God (see 1 Cor. 3:18), while simply being "taken" to heaven can miss this right teaching. I think Augustine would have sung the older version.

all of life, including our intellectual endeavors, has a telos as part of the very nature of things. This "nature" of things is divinely given, and God creates us as beings ordered to God.[33] Our lives—whether we consciously recognize it or not—are going somewhere. And if that is the case, if *all* of life is viewed against the landscape of a certain telos or goal, then even apparently nontheological matters (such as music, history, mathematics) have their ultimate end in God himself. There ultimately are no "nontheological matters."

This extends to the non-Christian as well, of course, since his or her life is one of the stories being lived out against the backdrop of God's larger and all-encompassing story. And perhaps we now come up against why the history of the modern mind is a history of nihilism, skepticism, and intellectual dead ends. While not all persons may confess Christ as Lord, they certainly live their lives in a world created, sustained, and governed by the triune God of Holy Scripture. Thus when non-Christians think, theorize, and deliberate as if they live in a world *not* governed and guided, it follows that there will be some type of "cognitive dissonance" between their intellectual life and the world as it really is.

Conclusion

At the end of the day, should we be surprised at the confusion about knowledge in the modern era? An age that began with high hopes has been unable to sustain its aspirations and confidence. But this should not shock us. The premodern era in its Christian form offered the world an understanding of the intellectual life that framed all of thought within an eschatological vision of God. There was a telos

---

[33]Wright's multivolume series on New Testament theology (from Fortress Press, with three volumes completed) comes to mind, as well as Milbank, *Theology and Social Theory*.

for human existence and thought that informed and sustained the intellectual life, infusing this life with a beautiful expectation of meeting God face-to-face. All that we are, think, and know in the present finds its culmination in that vision. If Christians could recover this compelling vision of where we are headed, we might see a genuine, gospel-centered renewal of the intellectual life in our own day. Our problem, as James V. Schall has noted, is that we "live in a culture dominated by a lower vision."[34]

Augustine offers one of the best theological examples of how Christians might recover a meaningful and fruitful life of the mind. Indeed, he construes the intellectual life in a gospel-centered and eschatologically oriented manner. While Alasdair MacIntyre a number of years ago quipped that we might have to wait out the new Dark Ages until a new Saint Benedict emerges,[35] I suspect what we most need is a new Saint Augustine—and with him, an understanding of the intellectual life that takes as its ultimate end the eschatological vision of God.

---

[34]James V. Schall, *On the Unseriousness of Human Affairs: Teaching, Writing, Playing, Believing, Lecturing, Philosophizing, Singing, Dancing* (Wilmington, DE: Intercollegiate Studies Institute, 2001), 89.
[35]This is found in the closing page of MacIntyre's *After Virtue: A Study in Moral Theory*, 2nd ed. (Notre Dame, IN: University of Notre Dame Press, 1984), 263.

Human minds are obscured by familiarity with darkness, which covers them in a night of sins and bad habits, and are unable to perceive with the clarity and purity proper to reason.

AUGUSTINE

But since the mind, itself, though naturally capable of reason and intelligence, is disabled by besotting and inveterate vices not merely from delighting and abiding in, but even from tolerating His unchangeable light, until it has been gradually healed, and renewed, and made capable of such felicity, it had, in the first place, to be impregnated with faith, and so purified.

AUGUSTINE

To doubt the existence of God would be an act of sheer irrationality, for it would mean that my reason had become unhinged from its bond with real being. Yet in knowing God I am deeply aware that my relation to Him has been damaged, that disorder has resulted in my mind, and that it is I who obstruct knowledge of God by getting in between Him and myself, as it were.

THOMAS F. TORRANCE

All our intellectual, aesthetic and moral endeavours fail unless they take place in due repentance and subordination to the truth.

COLIN E. GUNTON

3

Understanding and the Cross

We started this book with a fundamental question: What is the link between the Christian faith and the intellectual life, between the gospel and the mind? In chapter 1 we explored the importance of creation and history. We suggested that without a notion of a created order it is hard to account for the possibility of understanding, and that the Christian faith encourages attention to the past, to a history worth remembering. In chapter 2 we observed that historically the Christian understanding of reality affirms that all of life finds its meaning in a telos or goal—the vision of God—and when this overarching telos is lost, accounting for a meaningful intellectual life becomes a hopeless endeavor. Now in chapter 3 we focus on the Christian gospel itself, particularly the atonement, but not to the exclusion of the incarnation and the resurrection. In short, we ask what indeed does the Christian gospel have to do with the life of the mind?

Augustine and Faith Seeking Understanding
Studies of Christian approaches to learning and knowledge commonly introduce the notion of "faith seeking understanding." Both Augustine and Anselm of Canterbury (1033–1109) were advocates of this approach, and it will never be far from view in this chapter.

What exactly does this slogan mean?[1] First, when Augustine speaks of faith seeking understanding, he is talking about understanding God. To come to know God we must first have faith in Christ, and it is through this faith in Christ that we are progressing toward one day seeing God face-to-face, thereby coming to a fuller (but not exhaustive) understanding of God. Thus, we have faith as we walk as pilgrims toward a fuller understanding in that future vision Paul described in 1 Corinthians 13:12. So, faith seeking understanding assumes what is often called a redemptive-historical understanding of the Bible and history. We are living in and participating in God's overarching story and sovereign plan. Augustine writes about this:

> Understanding refers to everlasting sight, while faith in tempo-
> ral things as a kind of cradle is, so to say, nourishing little ones
> on milk; now, however, we are walking by faith and not by sight
> (2 Cor. 5:7), but unless we walk by faith, we shall never be able
> to reach the sight which does not pass away but endures, when
> with our understanding purified we cleave to Truth.[2]

---

[1]In this section I have reworked some material from my "Augustine" chapter in *Shapers of Christian Orthodoxy: Engaging with Early and Medieval Theologians*, ed. Bradley G. Green (Nottingham: Apollos, 2010), 271–72.
[2]Augustine *On Christian Doctrine* 2.17 (*Teaching Christianity*, The Works of Saint Augustine: A Translation for the 21st Century, trans. Edmund Hill, ed. John E. Rotelle [Brooklyn, NY: New City, 1992]). The New City Press edition loosely translates the original title of *De doctrina Christiania*. Elsewhere I have retained the traditional English title, *On Christian Doctrine*.

We see in this quotation two of the key themes of this book: the notion of a telos or goal to history (chap. 2), and the notion that to truly see God our minds must be purified (chap. 3). It is this notion of the mind needing to be purified or transformed by the cross that is at the heart of this chapter. But first we need to avoid a potential misunderstanding.

Augustine is not somehow setting faith and understanding in opposition to one another. His approach is not faith *versus* understanding, or understanding *versus* faith. Neither is Augustine playing faith against reason, as if faith were noncognitive. Augustine teaches that believing is always preceded by thinking:

> Everything which is believed should be believed after thought has preceded; although even belief itself is nothing else than to think with assent. For it is not every one who thinks that believes, since many think in order that they may not believe; but everybody who believes, thinks—both thinks in believing, and believes in thinking.[3]

When I affirm the fundamental appropriateness of faith seeking understanding, with Augustine I mean that all knowledge is ultimately rooted in faith commitments. It is not the case that knowledge of *God* requires faith while knowledge of *other things* (such as knowledge of the desk at which I'm writing) happens *naturally* apart from faith. Two interrelated convictions reside in this book: (1) "faith seeking understanding" means that *all* knowledge rests on certain faith commitments that are at the heart of knowing; and (2) "faith seeking understanding" implies that faith for the Christian is always striving to understand, to flesh out what has already been initially believed.

---

[3]Augustine *Predestination of the Saints* 5 (Vernon J. Bourke, *The Essential Augustine*, 2nd ed. [Indianapolis: Hackett, 1974], 22).

Thus, while the phrase "faith seeking understanding" originally had to do narrowly with understanding God, I am extending it to knowledge more generally. In all of our knowledge—both of God and of the created order—we truly know only when we know in a faith-seeking-understanding way. As God's creatures in God's world, we truly know only when we know in light of who God is and what he has spoken to us.

How do we come to know things in light of who God is and what he has spoken? How do we begin to "think God's thoughts after him," as Johannes Kepler put it? While we know in part because we are created in the image of God, much of what we can know of God and his world comes only through minds transformed by the gospel. And the path of gospel transformation is a road that travels through the reality of sin.

The Will, Sin, and the Possibility of Knowledge
The relationship between sin and knowledge is a theme found in the Old Testament, in Jesus, in Paul and other New Testament writings, and in numerous thinkers throughout church history. Contemporary thinkers continue to delineate the link between decadence and the disintegration of knowledge. Eugen Rosenstock-Huessy, for example, observes that "decadence is the disease of liberalism today," and he posits that "lack of faith is a synonym for decadence."[4]

Christians have historically contended that the cross is at the center of the Christian faith. While various Christian traditions have struggled to articulate all that happened on the cross, no serious Christian can doubt that the cross of Christ is central. Given that centrality, it is appropriate to ask how the cross relates to the intellectual life. What are

---

[4]Eugen Rosenstock-Huessy, *Speech and Reality* (Norwich, VT: Argo, 1988), 12–13.

the implications of the reality of the cross for the life of the mind?

Contemporary philosopher Alasdair MacIntyre offers stimulating discussion in which he asks how persons should think and act amid the death throes following the Enlightenment. MacIntyre argues that the reason for the impasse of so much of modern thought is that modernity, and modern ethical reflection in particular, utilizes certain terms, convictions, and arguments dislocated from their historical place within a particular moral and ethical tradition. MacIntyre contends that such ethical and moral assertions were once rooted in specific traditions and understandings, but are now being argued apart from their origin and therefore apart from their historic meaning.

The reason two sides in many contemporary arguments—such as abortion or just-war theory—never seem able to persuade the other, is that they are putting forward ethical claims that are now rooted in completely different, and in MacIntyre's view, *incommensurate*, traditions. And most of the time, MacIntyre suggests, the interlocutors are not very aware of the traditions from which their own ethical arguments and convictions have sprung. Moreover, MacIntyre argues that the "liberal project" of universal rationality and of "presuppositionless" reasoning is fallacious and fantastic—it is a fantasy that does not work. People properly, and inescapably, predicate and argue from within one intellectual tradition or another. The tradition of choice for MacIntyre is Aristotelianism (and ultimately Thomism, in recent years). While evangelicals may not want to make Aristotle (or Thomas) their hero, MacIntyre's thesis is nonetheless helpful for Christians who are casting around for nonmodernist ways to construe living, believing, and acting in the world. Thus, in his insightful analysis of the modern university, MacIntyre comments:

> Moral enquiry without some kind of presupposed prior agreements is barren. And since the moral diversity of contemporary society and the presuppositions of the liberal [read "modern"] university combine to make such agreements impossible, it is unsurprising that moral philosophy has declined in its relative importance in the modern curriculum.[5]

Taking our cue from MacIntyre at this point, we might expand his argument and contend that not simply "moral enquiry" but indeed intellectual life as a whole can only proceed where there is a commitment to a unifying vision of reality—in explicitly Christian terms, a Christian vision and understanding of the world.

As this relates to the gospel and the life of the mind, Christians in the modern or postmodern world intuitively cast around for helpful, meaningful, and perhaps apologetical ways to make sense of the world. Christians need to ask how we might construe the intellectual life in ways that are redemptive, holistic, and enduring. The life of the mind, the act of knowing, is not a morally or spiritually neutral endeavor. To truly think God's thoughts after him, indeed to truly think in terms of a coherent view of the whole, we must think in a way consonant with the reality that this is God's world as understood on God's terms. Christians need not be embarrassed or timid about speaking about the intellectual life in explicitly Christian terms and categories. And if this really is the case, we need to ask about the relationship between the cross and the intellectual life.

---

[5]Alasdair MacIntyre, *Three Rival Versions of Moral Enquiry: Encyclopedia, Genealogy, and Tradition* (Notre Dame, IN: University of Notre Dame Press, 1990), 227.

It is striking that although the cross is indeed central to a Christian vision of the world, little is written on this relationship today. Until recently, the Christian faith has consistently throughout its history generated a passion for the intellectual life, as a brief survey will show. We begin with the New Testament.

The Cross and the Mind in the New Testament
Boethius (ca. 475–525), writing from a prison cell when, apparently, the barbarian king who had invaded the Holy Roman Empire no longer thought he was loyal, penned his renowned work *The Consolation of Philosophy*. In it he says, "In spite of a clouded memory, the mind seeks its own good, though like a drunkard it cannot find the path home."[6]

Boethius captures a central truth. We do have "clouded memories," and in a sense we do seek our own good, even if our mental "drunkenness" keeps us from what is truly the good. Indeed, Augustine teaches that all people seek pleasure, or their own good. But apart from God's guidance, we all generally make one of two errors: we either (1) seek and love the wrong thing (what will not in fact bring us happiness or be good for us) or (2) seek and love the right thing, but in the wrong way or in an inordinate manner.

In Boethius's powerful metaphor, the mind not redeemed by the cross is like a drunk who is unable to find his way home. Why are we mentally "drunks"? Traditionally, Christians have pointed to the reality of human sin.

Scripture makes it abundantly clear that sin affects our noetic (knowing) faculties and abilities. Paul says, for example, that the Colossians were once "hostile in mind"

---

[6]Boethius, *The Consolation of Philosophy*, rev. ed., trans. Victor Watts (London: Penguin Books, 1999), 3.3 (49).

(Col. 1:21). In Romans 8 he speaks of the unregenerate as having minds set "on the things of the flesh" (v. 5). The unregenerate mind is "hostile to God, for it does not submit to God's law; indeed, it cannot" (v. 7). Again, in Ephesians, Paul says, "Among [various sins] we all once lived in the passions of our flesh, carrying out the desires of the body *and the mind* [lit., "thoughts"—*dianoiōn; dianoia*, sg.], and were by nature children of wrath, like the rest of mankind" (Eph. 2:3). In Romans 1, when Paul catalogs a long chain of sins that follow from suppressing the knowledge of God (v. 18), he adds, "And since they [those who continually suppress the knowledge of God] did not see fit to acknowledge God, God gave them up to a debased mind to do what ought not to be done" (v. 28). When comparing the old and new covenants in 2 Corinthians 3–4, speaking of Jews who have not confessed Christ as Lord, Paul says, "But their minds [*noēmata; noēma*, sg.] were hardened. For to this day, when they read the old covenant, that same veil remains unlifted, because only through Christ is it taken away" (2 Cor. 3:14). Paul is here referring to the "same" veil that covered Moses' face when he came down from Mount Sinai, thus keeping the people from seeing the glory of God. What is fascinating in terms of our discussion is Paul's explanation that this "veil" remains unlifted because it is removed in Christ.

Without trying to navigate the exact nature of the details in Paul's biographical sketch in Romans 7, we should note that when speaking of this "war" within himself, Paul writes, "I see in my members another law waging war against the law *of my mind* [*nous*] and making me captive to the law of sin that dwells in my members" (Rom. 7:23). Sin is at war with the mind. The mind is not sequestered from the reality of sin.[7]

John Calvin taught that the mind is a factory of idols, and he had good scriptural warrant for such a claim.[8] Not only is our knowing ability *limited* (because we are *created*, not the Creator), but our knowing ability is also *injured* or *corrupted* by sin. According to Paul in Romans 1:18–25, the bent of sinful man is to worship the creation instead of the Creator. Man *will* worship, and if man does not worship the triune God, he will create idols to worship. Since a Christian vision of the intellectual life ultimately realizes that there is a Christian way of knowing, it is important that Christians recognize that our knowing is not somehow neutral. Even our knowing is caught up in sin, and this must be acknowledged as we forge a Christian understanding of the mind.

Every aspect of our being, including the intellectual life, is caught up in the ugliness of sin, seeking to escape the lordship of Christ. But as Abraham Kuyper said famously, "No single piece of our mental world is to be hermetically sealed off from the rest, and there is not a square inch in the whole domain of our human existence over which Christ, who is Sovereign over *all*, does not cry: 'Mine!'"[9] Giving

---

[7]In commenting on the *nous* word group in the New Testament, G. Harder notes, "The whole group of words is associated more firmly with the will, and the understanding spoken of is an understanding of God and his will in salvation, an understanding of the word in scripture and preaching. Understanding itself becomes a disposition, an attitude, and thus a standpoint of faith." G. Harder, "Reason, Mind, Understanding," in *New International Dictionary of New Testament Theology*, ed. Colin Brown, 4 vols. (Carlisle: Paternoster, 1992), 3:123.
[8]See John Calvin, *Institutes of the Christian Religion*, ed. John T. McNeill, trans. Ford Lewis Battles (Philadelphia: Westminster, 1960), 1.11.8. Calvin writes, "For as rashness and superficiality are joined to ignorance and darkness, scarcely a single person has ever been found who did not fashion for himself an idol or specter in place of God. Surely, just as waters boil up from a vast, full spring, so does an immense crowd of gods flow forth from the human mind, while each one, in wandering about with too much license, wrongly invents this or that about God himself" (1.5.12).
[9]Abraham Kuyper, inaugural lecture at the Free University of Amsterdam, October 20, 1880, quoted in *Abraham Kuyper: A Centennial Reader*, ed. James D. Bratt (Grand Rapids: Eerdmans, 1998), 488.

no ground to the pretense of autonomy from Christ, any Christian understanding of the intellectual life should strive toward "take every thought captive to obey Christ" (2 Cor. 10:5).

At the heart of the Christian faith stands the gospel of Jesus Christ—his death, burial, and resurrection for sinners. The second person of the Trinity took on human flesh, suffered on the cross for our sins, and was raised for our justification. Redemption *accomplished* in the past is *applied* to the sinner in the present when he or she believes.[10] At the heart of God's redemptive purposes is the renewing of the human mind. We have mentioned that Scripture speaks repeatedly of the non-Christian mind as hostile to God (Rom. 8:7; Col. 1:21), of how the non-Christian mind is death (Rom. 8:6), and of how the non-Christian can be spoken of as actually an enemy of God (Rom. 5:10). For the redeemed sinner, there is a radical change in one's orientation, and this radical change results in the continual renewing of the mind.

Just as the Christian is a new person at conversion (2 Cor. 5:17), but continues to grow in grace (Phil. 2:12–13), so the Christian has a new mind at conversion, but continues to be transformed in his or her mind throughout life (Rom. 12:1–2). Redemption in its fullest sense is both something

---

[10]Cf. John Murray, *Redemption Accomplished and Applied* (Grand Rapids: Eerdmans, 1955). By speaking of a telos under the rubric of redemption, I am not denying that there is a telos in creation, and I am not trying to drive a wedge between creation and redemption (as if a telos only sprang into existence with redemption). Creation and redemption are both part of God's sovereign plan, and there is both continuity and discontinuity between them. Colin Gunton has expressed concern that Western theological thought, due largely to the influence of Augustine, has tended to divorce creation from redemption. Among his many writings, see Colin Gunton, "The Doctrine of Creation," in *The Cambridge Companion to Christian Doctrine*, ed. Colin E. Gunton (Cambridge: Cambridge University Press, 1997), 141–57; Gunton, *The One, The Three and the Many: God, Creation and the Culture of Modernity* (Cambridge: Cambridge University Press, 1994); Gunton, *The Triune Creator: A Historical and Systematic Study* (Grand Rapids: Eerdmans, 1998). I offer a critique of Gunton in my, *Colin Gunton and the Failure of Augustine: The Theology of Colin Gunton in Light of Augustine* (Eugene, OR: Wipf and Stock, 2010).

applied to us at a particular moment (it is punctiliar) and an ongoing process (it is progressive). Central to a Christian vision of the intellectual life is the affirmation that God is constantly renewing the mind of his children: Paul says to the Romans, "Do not be conformed to this world, but be transformed by the renewal of your mind, that by testing you may discern what is the will of God, what is good and acceptable and perfect" (Rom. 12:2).

Note in this text that the Romans are commanded to "*be* transformed.*"* While certainly this transformation is God's act, it is simultaneously the act of the Christian. In the rest of Romans, based on the gospel set forth in the preceding chapters, we are commanded to think *this* way instead of *that*, to do *this* deed instead of *that* one, to make *this* decision instead of *that* decision. A similar concurrence of God's work and ours is seen in such passages as Philippians 2:12–13. The Philippians are commanded to "work out your salvation with fear and trembling." Is Paul teaching salvation by works? Not at all; in the next verse he continues, "for it is God who works in you, both to will and to work for his good pleasure." Paul can teach that *we* must work out our salvation while in the very same act it is *God* who is at work in us.

The renewing of the mind is a common theme in Paul's writings. In Ephesians 4, for example, Paul speaks of Gentiles who walk "in the futility of their minds" (v. 17), who are "are darkened in their understanding" (v. 18). The redeemed, on the other hand, have been taught Christ, and should thus "put off your old self" (v. 22), "be renewed in the spirit of your minds, and . . . put on the new self" (vv. 23–24). While Christians are *already* new creatures in Christ (2 Cor. 5:17), notice that Paul commands his readers in Ephesus to "*be* renewed in the spirit of your minds," and to "*put on* the new self." There is both an *already* and a *not-yet* reality to the life of the Christian—including the renewing of the mind.

As evangelicals proclaim the centrality of the gospel, it is proper to ask how the gospel is central to a Christian understanding of the mind. We have noted above that unregenerate persons are dead in sin, and that this state is often portrayed in terms of the mind and thoughts. We've seen that Colossians 1:21 speaks of being enemies of Christ in our minds, and that Ephesians 2:3 tells of the *thoughts* of the sinful nature. And we have shown that redemption includes the transformation of the mind, according to Romans 12:2. In addition, 1 Corinthians 2:16 says that "we have the mind of Christ," and Ephesians 4:23 speaks of being made new "in the spirit of your mind." Clearly, redemption of the whole person includes the transformation of the mind, and ultimately this redemption of the mind springs from the gospel of reconciliation. Our intellectual development as Christians should always be seen as part of our being conformed to the image of Christ (Rom. 8:29), something rooted in and proceeding from the cross. Though the Colossians passage noted above describes the unregenerate person's hostility of the mind, the very next verse declares that Christ "has now reconciled [you] in his body of flesh by his death, in order to present you holy and blameless and above reproach before him" (Col. 1:22). It is Christ's death on the cross that reconciles us—including our minds—to God.[11]

---

[11]We should note that while this essay is mainly focused on the cross, the New Testament also speaks of the centrality of all of the "stages" of Christ's work. Thus, in 1 John 5:20 John can speak of the connection between Christ's incarnation and our understanding. John writes, "And we know that the Son of God has come and has given us understanding [*dianoia*], so that we may know him who is true; and we are in him who is true, in his Son Jesus Christ. He is the true God and eternal life." On a different note, it is worth noting that in his postresurrection appearance in Luke 24, when Christ encounters two of his disciples on the road to Emmaus, Luke can write of Jesus, "Then he opened their minds [*nous*, sg.] to understand the Scriptures" (Luke 24:45; cf. 24:31).

Christ and the Life of the Mind in Christian History
One of the Christian faith's great insights is that nothing
lies outside the good and providential workings of God. This
includes the life of the mind. Some of the church's earliest
and most profound thinkers made the connection between
the reality of God and the possibility of human understanding. We may cite several key examples.[12]

Augustine
We saw earlier that in his classic work *The Trinity*, Augustine
devotes two books largely to the atoning work of Christ. In
that treatment, Augustine is compelled to offer a polemic
against the Neoplatonists, who held that the goal of man was
to ascend to "the One" (God), and that this was achieved
by the will and action of man. Augustine counters that the
only way one can *ascend* to God is if God has *descended*
to us. Christ has, in fact, descended for us and died for us,
and if we are in him, we ascend with him to the presence
of God. Augustine writes, "Christ is the Principle by whose
incarnation we are purified. . . . But the incarnation of the
unchangeable Son of God, whereby we are saved, [enables
us] to reach the things we believe, or in part understand."[13]
Not only the incarnation, but the cross too is necessary. If
we are to truly see God (1 Cor. 13:12), then we (our minds)
must be purified: "The only thing to cleanse the wicked and
the proud is the blood of the just man and the humility of
God; to contemplate God, which by nature we are not, we

---

[12]There are other historical examples that could be raised here. From the Reformation, Luther's
distinction between the theologian of the cross and the theologian of glory comes to mind.
See "Theses for Heidelberg Disputation," in *Martin Luther: Selections From His Writings*, ed.
John Dillenberger (New York: Anchor Books Doubleday, 1962), 502–3 (especially numbers
20, 21, 22, 24).
[13]Augustine, *The City of God*, trans. Marcus Dods (New York: Modern Library, 1950), 20.24,
29.

would have to be cleansed by him who became what by nature we are and what by sin we are not."[14]

Augustine illustrates: Some persons have been able to "direct the keen gaze of their intellects" in such a way as to achieve at least a small glimpse of "the light of unchanging truth," but many find they cannot achieve such a task. Should the Christian place himself on the side of the few who can achieve such a daunting task? Not at all. Augustine explains, "What good does it do a man who is so proud that he is ashamed to climb aboard the wood, what good does it do him to gaze afar on the home country across the sea?" He continues, "And what harm does it do a humble man if he cannot see it from such a distance, but is coming to it nonetheless on the wood the other disdains to be carried by?"[15] In short, there is no shame in admitting one's weaknesses and embracing the cross. Why "gaze afar" when the "wood," the cross, is the only way by which we can reach the "home country"?

Augustine's analogy is worth pondering. Even the man of keen mind does not really make it to the homeland. He can only see the homeland from afar. The options are not (1) having a keen mind and thereby being in the presence of the One, and (2) not having a keen mind and thus needing the cross. Rather, the *only* way to reach the homeland is through the cross, and the keenest of minds will at most gaze from afar on the homeland of the presence of God.

Augustine is clear that while the vision of God is our goal, our current state impedes such a goal: "To sum up then: we were incapable of grasping eternal things, and weighed down by the accumulated dirt of our sins, which we had

---

[14]Augustine, *The Trinity*, trans. Edmund Hill, The Works of Saint Augustine (Brooklyn, NY: New City, 1991), 4.4.
[15]Ibid.

collected by our love of temporal things, and which had become almost a natural growth on our mortal stock; so we needed purifying."[16] The means of this purification is the person and the work of Christ. It would not be appropriate to "pass from being among the things that originated to eternal things, unless the eternal allied himself to us in our originated condition, and so provided us with a bridge to his eternity."[17] Thus, the Word became flesh for our salvation, and through this fleshly Word we are led to see the eternal Word:

> There he was, manifest before their eyes surely; then it can only mean that he was offering the flesh which the Word had been made in the fullness of time as the object to receive our faith; but that the Word itself, *through whom all things had been made* (Jn. 1:3), was being kept for the contemplation in eternity of minds now purified through faith.[18]

As one commentator has summarized Augustine's point, "There can be no *intellectus* [understanding] *apart from the concrete sacrificial act of Christ.*"[19] Indeed, it is the gospel that is at the heart of a genuine understanding and the true intellectual life, which has its ultimate end in seeing God face-to-face.

Hugh of St. Victor and Richard of St. Victor
Hugh of St. Victor (1096–1141) was abbot of the Abbey of St. Victor, Paris. He is called the "other Augustine" (*alter Augustinus*) because he is a prominent example of Augus-

[16]Ibid., 4.24.
[17]Ibid.
[18]Ibid., 4.26.
[19]Earl C. Muller, "Rhetorical and Theological Issues in the Structuring of Augustine's *De Trinitate*," in *Cappadocian Fathers, Greek Authors after Nicaea, Augustine, Donatism and Pelagianism*, ed. Elizabeth A. Livingstone, Studia Patristica 27 (Leuven: Peeters, 1993), 359. Emphasis original.

tinian thought in the Middle Ages. He is known in particular for his systematic theology *De sacramentis* ("On the Sacraments of the Christian Faith," written around 1134) and his *Didascalicon*, a manual on reading and the liberal arts (written in the late 1120s). Much could be said of Hugh, and he has been called "the most influential theologian of the twelfth century."[20] He is worthy of careful study for any number of reasons, but here I am simply concerned with how he—like Augustine—construes the knowing process in a radically theological way.

Hugh gives more sustained attention to the outworking of the liberal arts than does Augustine (as far as we can tell from their surviving writings). In that connection Hugh writes, "The eye of the heart must be cleansed by the study of virtue, so that it may thereafter see clearly for the investigation of truth in the theoretical arts."[21] Note that when the eye of the heart is cleansed, only then can a person really grasp the "truth" of the arts. This is a radically Augustinian—and biblical—theme. We can know things only when we know via a mind transformed by the gospel. The life of the mind is a subset of the life of discipleship, and we are truly engaging in the intellectual life—at least in its fullest sense—only when we have been transformed by the cross of Christ.

Hugh's successor, Richard of St. Victor (died AD 1173), likewise affirms Christ's role in the knowing process. Richard says, "How great is the difference between teaching in which earthly things are taught and teaching in which heav-

---

[20]Adolf von Harnack, *History of Dogma*, 7 vols. (London, 1899), 6:44; quoted in the Roy J. Deferrari's introduction to Hugh's *Sacraments of the Christian Faith* (Eugene, OR: Wipf and Stock, 2007), ix.
[21]Hugh of St. Victor, *Didascalicon*, trans. Jerome Taylor (New York: Columbia University Press, 1991), 154. For Hugh the "Theoretical Arts" are theology, mathematics, and physics. Under mathematics come the traditional *quadrivium* (the "four ways" or four latter liberal arts): arithmetic, music, geometry, astronomy.

enly things are taught—and certainly not without Christ since without Truth neither the one nor the other is understood." While Richard makes a distinction between "earthly things" and "heavenly things," *neither* realm is understood apart from Christ. Indeed, as Richard continues, "it is Christ who teaches both."[22] A little later Richard says that "Christ teaches me concerning exterior things or concerning my self."[23] Speaking of contemplation (the final state of the intellectual life for Richard), he stresses the role of grace in reaching that state. "For indeed," he says, "the mind by its own activity can never attain to such grace. This gift is from God; it is not a reward to man. But without doubt no person receives such and so much grace without a mighty effort and burning longing."[24]

Both these great Victorines, Hugh and Richard, emphasize the moral state of the knower. In short, knowledge is difficult, if not impossible, for the person whose will is misdirected, or for the person who is not led by Christ, who is the truth. Richard can write, "Whoever thirsts to see his God—let him wipe his mirror, let him cleanse his spirit. . . . When the mirror has been wiped and gazed into for a long time, a kind of splendor of divine light begins to shine in it and a great beam of unexpected vision appears in his eyes."[25]

Bonaventure

Bonaventure (1217–1274), who taught at the University of Paris, in his *The Journey of the Mind to God* construes the

[22] Richard of St. Victor, *The Twelve Patriarchs, The Mystical Ark, Book Three of the Trinity*, trans. Grover A. Zinn, Classics of Western Spirituality (New York: Paulist Press, 1979), 138.
[23] Ibid.
[24] Ibid., 131.
[25] Ibid., 130.

knowing process in a radically Christ-centered way. We need cite just one excerpt:

> After our mind has beheld God outside itself through and in vestiges of Him, and within itself through and in an image of Him, and above itself through the similitude of the divine Light shining above us and in the divine Light itself in so far as it is possible in our state as wayfarer and by the effort of our own mind, and when at last the mind has reached the sixth step, where it can behold in the first and highest Principle and in the Mediator of God and men, Jesus Christ, things the like of which cannot possibly be found among creatures, and which transcend all acuteness of the human intellect—when the mind has done all this, it must still, in beholding these things, transcend and pass over, not only this visible world, but even itself. In this passing over, Christ is the way and the door; Christ is the ladder and the vehicle, being, as it were, the Mercy-Seat above the Ark of God and the mystery which has been hidden from eternity.[26]

Thomas Aquinas

While Thomas Aquinas (ca. 1225–1274) does not give the same attention to the relationship between the cross and the intellectual life as do others, he has penetrating insights into the nature of knowledge. It is fairly common to highlight Aquinas's differences with Augustine. For instance, whereas Augustine believed that God must illumine the human mind in *every* act of cognition, Aquinas denies that a special divine illumination is needed for man to know at least natural things. But upon reading him, one sees all sorts of fascinating parallels between Aquinas and Augustine.

Although a special divine illumination is needed to know *supernatural* things, *every* act of knowing is undergirded and brought about by God's providential working, Aquinas

---

[26]Bonaventure, *The Journey of the Mind to God*, trans. Philotheus Boehner (Indianapolis: Hackett, 1993), 7 (37).

believes: "Therefore in any knowledge of truth the human mind stands in need of divine *operations*, but in knowing natural things it does not require a new light, but only its own motion and direction, although in other things it needs a new illumination."[27] He continues, "Similarly intellect cannot know any truth without divine movement, but it can without the infusion of a new light, although not those things which exceed natural knowledge." And finally, "It should be said that by the very fact that God by conserving in us the natural light causes and directs it to seeing, it is manifest that the grasp of truth ought to be especially ascribed to him, just as artistic activity is attributed to the artist rather than to his chisel."[28]

Thomas is also helpful in his emphasis on *proportion*, or what is proper. For example, in speaking of knowledge of God or of divine things, he says, "The human mind should always be seeking to know God more and more according to its manner."[29]

Conclusion

As we engage in the intellectual task, we must seek to take all thoughts captive to the obedience of Christ. We should ultimately see all endeavors of our minds as a subset of discipleship. The intellectual life should be a life grounded in the cross, that is, rooted in and flowing from the gospel. Indeed, if Paul and Augustine are right that the knowledge of God—and ultimately all knowledge—is dependent on the reality of Christ and his cross, then to fail to embrace the centrality of a gospel-centered intellectual life is to attempt

---

[27]Thomas Aquinas, "Theology, Faith and Reason. On Boethius *on the Trinity*, 1–2," in *Thomas Aquinas: Selected Writings*, ed. Ralph McInerny (London: Penguin Books, 1998), 113. Emphasis mine.
[28]Ibid., 114.
[29]Ibid., 128.

brazenly to approach God on our own terms. Biblically and historically, that is not wise—to say the least. If, as C. S. Lewis says, with every action or thought we are becoming either more heavenly or more hellish, then we must take seriously the role of the cross for the intellectual life. To become more heavenly creatures, and not hellish, is to be about the task of embracing the lordship of Christ over the life of the mind at every turn. Borrowing a Reformation slogan, we might say that if the Christian church is *semper reformanda* ("always to be reformed"), then the Christian mind is *semper capiens* ("always taking captive").[30] May we as Christians passionately and truly embrace the cross as we seek to glorify God in all that we do—including our intellectual deliberations.

---

[30]I have not attempted in this section to tackle all the issues related to faith, rationality, and epistemology. An important text is Alvin Plantinga and Nicholas Wolterstorff, *Faith and Rationality: Reason and Belief in God* (South Bend, IN: University of Notre Dame Press, 1983). Also see Paul Helm, *Faith and Understanding*, Reason and Religion (Grand Rapids: Eerdmans, 1997); Helm, ed., *Faith and Reason* (Oxford: Oxford University Press, 1999).

My impression is that we have seen, for perhaps a hundred and fifty years, a gradual increase in language that is either meaningless or destructive of meaning. And I believe that this increasing unreliability of language parallels the increasing disintegration, over the same period, of persons and communities.

WENDELL BERRY

We serve a talkative God, who does not even seem to be able to do without a library. In his service, we will be concerned for talk and libraries.

ROBERT JENSON

Cultures wish to avoid ultimate reality by taking refuge in linguistic games and theological systems, rather than facing external reality, which might just cause them to have to face the living God.

DOUGLAS F. KELLY

I am inclined to believe that when the language in common use in any country becomes irregular and depraved, it is followed by their ruin and degradation. For what do terms used without skill or meaning, which are at once corrupt and misapplied, denote but a people listless, supine, and ripe for servitude?

JOHN MILTON

4

Words, Language, and Modern Culture

There is an inextricable link between the Christian gospel and attentiveness to words.[1] The modern world has witnessed confusion about the nature of language and the

---

[1]Of all the chapters in this book, this chapter on language could have become the most technical. The world of literary theory, structuralism, poststructuralism/deconstruction, and the like is a wild intellectual realm that can consume all of one's mental energy. I am trying in this chapter to sketch out key themes and to offer readers a way to navigate some difficult issues. Readers who want to dig a bit deeper can turn to the footnotes where I discuss some of these issues at greater length. An extremely helpful recent book is Vern Sheridan Poythress, *In the Beginning Was the Word: Language—A God-Centered Approach* (Wheaton, IL: Crossway, 2009). Poythress's treatment of language is the most exhaustive that I am aware of, offering a biblical and systematic theology, of sorts, of language. At 410 pages, that excellent volume does more than I am trying to do in this chapter. Also very helpful is David Lyle Jeffrey, *People of the Book: Christian Identity and Literary Culture* (Grand Rapids: Eerdmans, 1996). Another seminal work is Kevin J. Vanhoozer, *Is There a Meaning in This Text? The Bible, the Reader, and the Morality of Literary Knowledge* (Grand Rapids: Zondervan, 1998). For a shorter treatment of deconstructionism, Louis Markos gives a strikingly clear and succinct summary of the issues in chapter 5 of his book *Lewis Agonistes: How C. S. Lewis Can Train Us to Wrestle with the Modern and Postmodern World* (Nashville: Broadman and Holman, 2003). Cf. the helpful work by Arthur M. Hunt III, *The Vanishing Word: The Veneration of Visual Imagery in the Postmodern World* (Wheaton, IL: Crossway, 2003).

THE GOSPEL AND THE MIND

possibility of meaning in communication. The Christian tradition (especially in the Gospel of John and the writings of Augustine) affirms a rich theology of language and communication, where words and signs are meaningful because they exist against the backdrop of a created order, because man as image bearer is a communicating and relational being, and because words and signs function in relation to the Word (Christ), who serves as the ground and goal of all language. At least one benefit of reading recent thinkers like Jacques Derrida is that he is honest enough to admit that without some sort of real and transcendent *logos*, meaningful communication is an impossibility. If anything, Christians can rejoice that they serve a communicating and speaking God, who has made us as image bearers capable of communicating, and that Christ—the Logos—is (in Augustine's words) "the Teacher" who illumines the human mind to know God, the world, and other persons.

Wordish Creatures

All persons, in some way, are fundamentally "wordish" creatures. We speak in words, write in words, type out words on our computers, and perhaps peck them out on a Blackberry or iPhone. The world is more than a collection of letters and words, of course. Visual arts, for example, capture dimensions of the created order in images and pictures. But humans are manifestly wordish folk.

While the use of words is a virtually universal reality among humans, only the Christian vision of God, man, and the world can explain why words matter. The Christian vision is the only one that can account for the meaningfulness of words. It not only helps us *recover* the possibility of the meaningfulness of language; the Christian vision of God, man, and the world also helps shape the way we handle language when we speak, write, or read.

We are wordish creatures because we were created by a wordish God, "a talkative God," as Robert Jenson describes him. "In his service, we will be concerned for talk and libraries. And some of us will have the privilege of spending a lot of time at that concern; if anyone wishes to call these 'Christian intellectuals,' there is no great reason to interdict the label."[2]

Walker Percy comments specifically on the value of reading:

> "If you do not learn to read, that is, read with pleasure, that is, make the breakthrough into the delight of reading—you are going to miss out." And I don't mean that you are going to miss out on books or being bookish. No, I mean that, no matter what you go into—law, medicine, computer science, housewifing, house-husbanding, engineering, whatever—you are going to miss out, you are not going to be first-class unless you've made this breakthrough. You are going to miss out, not only on your profession, but on the great treasure of your heritage, which is nothing less than Western civilization.[3]

Philosophers have continually come up against the importance of language as one of the unique realities of being human. Language allows people to accomplish great good, to do many admirable things, but also to accomplish great evil, to inflict astounding pain and harm on others. When language serves within a framework of transcendent realities and ultimate goals, it can be thought of in glorious terms. But when the modern world jettisoned transcendent

---

[2]Robert W. Jenson, *Essays in Theology of Culture* (Grand Rapids: Eerdmans, 1995), 168.
[3]Walker Percy, *Signposts in a Strange Land* (New York: Farrar, Straus and Giroux, 1991), 356. Percy first quotes a hypothetical speaker in this passage.

goals and causes, language came to be construed in quite a different manner.

Thomas Hobbes (1588–1679) is a helpful example. Hobbes affirmed that man is simply the aggregate of all his desires and impulses. A person may think he is free or that he is exercising intention in choosing this or that path. But when someone acts or decides or chooses, what are really acting or deciding or choosing are simply that person's desires and passions.[4] Thus, when he uses language, it is just one more tool for appeasing his desires and passions. As Thomas Gillespie explains, "For Hobbes humans are more powerful because they use language. Language enables humans to extend their sway over the world and thus to become extraordinarily dangerous to other human beings."[5]

Words, Cultures, and Community

Wendell Berry has observed that in recent times we have witnessed the collapse of communities along with the collapse of the meaning and practice of language. With genuinely penetrating insight, Berry writes, "Two epidemic illnesses of our time—upon both of which virtual indus-

---

[4]This line of thought is central to what Thomas Hobbes is doing in *Leviathan*, ed. Michael Oakeshott (New York: Touchstone, 1962). Hobbes's *Leviathan* was originally published in 1651.

[5]Thomas Gillespie, *The Theological Origins of Modernity* (Chicago: University of Chicago Press, 2008), 237. The Christian—who affirms the reality and fundamental goodness of the body—can agree with Hobbes that our desires and impulses are a constituent part of what it means to be human and what it means to act. However, the Christian parts with Hobbes on at least two key points. First, Hobbes did not have (or he ignored or denied) the resources to make moral judgments about particular actions; for Hobbes, we all follow our desires and impulses, and there can be no moral judgments on such actions. But the Christian believes that man is morally accountable for his actions, since all persons know God and his moral law (Romans 1), and we have full-orbed moral instruction in Holy Scripture. Second, we are more than simply a combination of impulses and desires. We are spiritual beings, and our actions are not simply the manifestation of impulses and passions. Man is a responsible, spiritual being, and human agency is genuine, morally accountable agency. As spiritual beings, we act because we choose and desire to act, even if our actions are shaped in significant ways by our bodily desires, impulses, and passions.

tries of cures have been founded—are the disintegration of communities and the disintegration of persons." Berry suggests that both of these "epidemic illnesses" are related to the concurrent disintegration of language in our day.

This chapter is concerned with the vexing issue of language and its apparent disintegration. Before considering what a Christian vision of the world contributes to our understanding of language, let us examine the tendency toward pessimism and nihilism concerning language in some circles today.

Language and the Modern Age

David Lyle Jeffrey documents a fascinating development in English language in the last two hundred years or more. He notes that during and since the Enlightenment one can trace a "radical ego-centering of discourse about persons."[6] For example, a number of terms have no adjectival uses before 1775 and few verbal uses thereafter, such that a word like *charming* would have been understood more as a verb before 1775 (a woman "charms" someone else) and more as an adjective since then (the woman *is* "charming"). This shift toward the adjective means that after 1775, *charming* essentially says something about the woman's effect on *me*, not about the woman herself. If Jeffrey is right, then the language of modernity itself testifies to the modernist emphasis on the virtually autonomous self. Jeffrey concludes,

> What I want to stress now is simply the fact that grammar—the hidden structure of language to which words are but flesh on the bones—is much slower to reflect a real change in values, but not at all invulnerable to change, and that changes at this

---

[6]David Lyle Jeffrey, *Houses of the Interpreter: Reading Scripture, Reading Culture* (Waco, TX: Baylor University Press, 2003), 200.

level are far more devastating, by means of their foundational nature and their hiddenness, than change at the level of the words we see on a page.[7]

Jeffrey's study suggests that even grammar is never ideologically or theologically neutral. Grammar both reflects an underlying vision and understanding of reality, and can shape one's vision and understanding. Thus, as George Steiner writes:

> The classic speech-construct, the centrality of the word, [is] informed by and expressive of both a hierarchic value-system, and the trope of transcendence. . . . An explicit grammar is an acceptance of order: it is a hierarchization, the more penetrating for being enforced so early in the individual life-span, of the forces and valuations prevailing in the body politic.[8]

Interestingly, Friedrich Nietzsche would agree with George Steiner at this point. In his *Will to Power*, Nietzsche argues that even to believe in the meaning of words, or in grammar, is to give evidence that one believes in God: "I'm afraid we're not rid of God, because we still believe in grammar."[9] In other words, even to have grammar is to have an explicit or implicit affirmation of a structure, order, and hierarchy that exists only if we live in a created world.

In his little book *Abuse of Language, Abuse of Power*,[10] Josef Pieper recognizes—though for reasons far different from Nietzsche's—that when language becomes dislocated from truth, some power or set of powers other than truth is

[7]Ibid., 201.
[8]George Steiner, *In Bluebeard's Castle* (London: Faber and Faber, 1971), 87–88, quoted in Jeffrey, *Houses of the Interpreter*, 277n2.
[9]Friedrich Nietzsche, *Twilight of the Idols: or How to Philosophize with a Hammer*, trans. Richard Polt (Indianapolis: Hackett, 1997), 21.
[10]Josef Pieper, *Abuse of Language, Abuse of Power*, trans. Lothar Krauth (1974; repr., San Francisco: Ignatius, 1988).

at work. For Pieper, this is an abuse of language and power. For Nietzsche, who acknowledges no ultimate truth, this is simply the way things are. Pieper speaks of "a timeless temptation that since the beginning of history has always required mankind's resistance and will require it forever."[11] He warns, "If the word becomes corrupted, human existence itself will not remain unaffected and untainted."[12] The word can be corrupted in two ways: there can be a "corruption of the relationship to reality," and there can be "corruption of communication."[13] That is, the corruption can be between the speaker and reality, or it can be in the communication itself.

Pieper recounts one of Plato's dialogs, in which Socrates is conversing with Gorgias. Socrates states that when sophisticated language is separated from truth, language is reduced to a means of exerting power. As Pieper describes it, "Sophisticated language, disconnected from the roots of truth, in fact pursues some ulterior motives, . . . it invariably turns into an instrument of power, something it has been, by its very nature, right from the start."[14] Indeed, when we are not guided by truth, we are always tempted to use language—and others—for our own ends: "Whoever, in other words, is in this [use of language] guided by something other than the truth—such a person, from that moment on, no longer considers the other as partner, as equal. In fact, he no longer respects the other as a human person."[15] In short, without a basis in truth, our language will be used to manipulate others—whom we no longer see or treat as human—for

---

[11]Ibid., 8.
[12]Ibid., 14.
[13]Ibid., 16.
[14]Ibid., 21.
[15]Ibid.

our own ends. We will no longer respect those around us as bearers of the *imago Dei*.

Like Berry, Pieper sees an organic link between the destruction of meaningful language and the destruction of community in our day. When truth is no longer center stage, Pieper says, "basically, what happens here is speech without a partner (since there is no other); such speech, in contradiction to the nature of language, intends not to communicate but to manipulate."[16] As Berry warned, the loss of language goes hand in hand with the loss of true community and meaningful culture. Pieper explains:

> Not just a specific sector is then endangered, such as the press, or television, or radio; no, the commonweal of all people is then threatened, since by necessity it functions through the medium of the word. Then we are faced, in short, with the threat that communication as such decays, that public discourse becomes detached from the notions of truth and reality.[17]

Pieper goes on to elaborate that when language is corrupted and becomes simply a means of manipulation and domination, then a culture is on the road to tyranny. In delineating this position, Pieper approves Plato's argument that the rise of Sophism means the rise of tyranny.[18] Pieper summarizes,

> This lesson, in a nutshell, says: the abuse of political power is fundamentally connected with the sophistic abuse of the word, indeed, finds in it the fertile soil in which to hide and grow and get ready, so much so that the latent potential of the totalitarian

---

[16]Ibid., 23.
[17]Ibid., 27.
[18]"Sophism" is the view that when we think, we are not really thinking about a reality outside ourselves. We are in a sense talking or thinking to ourselves. We simply have notions or ideas bumping around in our heads.

poison can be ascertained, as it were, by observing the symptom of the public abuse of language.[19]

It is important not to miss Pieper's key insights. In order to possess meaningful language, he argues, one must affirm that with language we are interacting with and relating to reality. Hence, meaningful language requires a meaningful understanding of reality—a meaningful *metaphysic*. This brings us back to the need for the Christian doctrine of creation: there is a real and good and ordered world that can be known and about which we speak. "The dignity of the word, to be sure, consists in this: through the word is accomplished what no other means can accomplish, namely, communication based on reality."[20]

When language is corrupted, we begin to lose hold of reality. We begin not to grasp the world as it is. Worse still, says Pieper, we begin to create a fictitious world.

We are reminded again of John Calvin's assertion early in the *Institutes of the Christian Religion* that human nature is a "perpetual factory of idols."[21] We do not simply *find* an idol—we actually *manufacture* idols to worship. Along similar lines, Pieper is saying that as we lose hold of reality, we create a fictitious reality to take its place. In short, we create a false world in which to live.[22]

---

[19]Pieper, *Abuse of Language*, 32–33.
[20]Ibid., 33.
[21]John Calvin, *Institutes of the Christian Religion*, ed. John T. McNeill, trans. Ford Lewis Battles (Philadelphia: Westminster, 1960), 1.11.8.
[22]Pieper, *Abuse of Language*, 34–35. Toward the end of his first essay, Pieper makes an assertion we might question. He says that the academy must be autonomous, free to follow truth and examine all things. But then he says that the academy must vigilantly oppose sophism and ideas that flow from sophism. It is hard to see how Pieper can affirm both the autonomy of the academy and the need to exclude sophism. Why should antisophism be an accepted (inviolable) position in a setting that seeks to be autonomous? This seems to be a genuine contradiction. There is a good case to be made for resisting sophism, but should the academy be open to having a chair of Sophist Studies, since this could very well be a necessary corollary of being autonomous? Or are there certain nonnegotiable convictions or premises in *any*

I have highlighted Wendell Berry's identification of a deep relationship between the decline of community and the decline of meaningful language. In view of that correlation, he proposes that "if one wishes to promote the life of language, one must promote the life of the community—a discipline many times more trying, difficult, and long than that of linguistics, but having at least the virtue of hopefulness."[23] And this brings us to the thesis of A. J. Conyers's last book, *The Listening Heart: Vocation and the Crisis of Modern Culture*.[24] There Conyers outlines what he sees as the key elements of modernity. For Conyers two key marks are the elevation of *choice* (in an individualistic sense) and the corresponding loss of a sense of *vocation* (a calling for our lives from outside us). Running throughout Conyers's book (though sometimes below the surface) is the recurring need for a true and enduring community in which this vocation can take place. In that respect *The Listening Heart* is a subtle apologetic for the necessity of the gospel if people are to recover from the vocationless desert of modernity.

When Berry laments the twin disintegration of language and of community, the question immediately arises, is there a way to recover? The way forward will be one in which the church is central, for the church is of course the ultimate, enduring—eternal—community in which we can find meaningful linguistic discourse, that is, the recovery of meaningful language.

academy, and it is wiser to confess one's institutional commitments up front than to pretend one does not have such commitments and to claim to be an autonomous academy?
[23]Wendell Berry, *Standing by Words: Essays by Wendell Berry* (San Francisco: North Point, 1983), 34.
[24]A. J. Conyers, *The Listening Heart: Vocation and the Crisis of Modern Culture* (Dallas, TX: Spence, 2006).

Toward the end of his essay "Standing by Words," Berry notes that ultimately a sentence is a means of limiting and expressing thought. We might add that in an era of skepticism about the possibility of meaning, we should therefore expect to see poor sentences. We should expect, in a post-Christian culture, to see poor grammar, poor composition. And this is of course exactly what we see. Some specialists, as Berry recounts, urge us to resist the "illegitimate tyranny of any kind of prescriptive grammar"; we should recognize "the absurdity of judging language 'on the bases of extra-linguistic considerations'" (i.e., moral, theological, or philosophical criteria).[25] But Berry is emphatic: without a theological understanding of man's place in the universe, we should expect to find incoherent thought and hence incoherent language.

Berry illustrates the needed theological perspective by means of an excerpt from John Milton's *Paradise Lost,* which upholds man's place in creation and his duty to honor God. What is lacking in the incoherence of modern thought is exactly what Milton affirms:

> the idea that humans have a place in Creation and that this place is limited by responsibility on the one hand and by humility on the other—or, in Milton's terms, by magnanimity and devotion. Without this precision of definition, this setting of bounds or ends to thought, we cannot mean, or say what we mean, or mean what we say; we cannot stand by our words because we cannot utter words that can be stood by; we cannot speak of our own actions as persons, or even as communities, but only of the actions of percentages, large organizations, concepts, historical trends, or the impersonal "forces" of destiny or evolution.[26]

---

[25]Berry, *Standing by Words*, 26.
[26]Ibid., 55.

Berry goes on to speak of "technological determinists," those who advocate the various "advances" of technology but have no overarching telos into which such realities might fit: "The technological determinists have tyranni-cal attitudes, and speak tyrannese, at least partly because their assumptions cannot produce a moral or a responsible definition of the human place in Creation." Note that, like Pieper, Berry contends that when the possibility of meaningful language is lost, tyranny rushes in. Bereft of a worldview that can affirm the reality of truth (and hence of coherent speech), technological determinists resort to "tyrannical" language ("tyrannese") to accomplish their purposes.

Richard Weaver concurs with Berry and even suggests that the stability and meaningfulness of language are rooted in the notion of covenant. As a professor of English and as a teacher of rhetoric, Weaver was concerned with the disintegration of communication in the modern age, and with the loss of a meaningful culture in our day. For Weaver, vital to the recovery of a meaningful culture is the recovery of knowledge, and an essential part of this recovery is the recovery of the importance and nature of language. Weaver quotes John Milton with approval, "We have never heard of any people or state which has not flourished in some degree of prosperity as long as their language has retained its elegance and its purity."[27]

Many witnesses (some lamenting, some enthusiastic) could testify to major shifts in the way language is viewed today. For someone new to these issues, it may seem tedious to ask what this or that person says about language. Don't we all

---

[27]John Milton, correspondence with Benedetto Bonomatthai, September 10, 1638, in *The Prose Works of John Milton*, 2 vols. (London, 1806), 1:xi-xii, quoted in Richard Weaver, "Relativism and the Use of Language," in *In Defense of Tradition: Collected Shorter Writings of Richard M. Weaver 1929-1963*, ed. Ted J. Smith III (Indianapolis: Liberty Fund, 2000), 389.

know intuitively that we can communicate with each other? This sentiment has the bottom line right—communication through language is real and possible. But it is important to understand the often-baffling criticisms of language, and the philosophical and theological assumptions that lie behind these criticisms. I also want to show that it is the Christian vision and understanding of reality that can *account for* what we tend to know in our hearts—that language is meaningful and communication is possible. Before developing that response, we need to explore some aspects of the current challenges to meaningful language by looking at an important trend, deconstructionism.

Derrida, Deconstructionism, and the Nature of Language
We turn to a particularly provocative thinker, Jacques Derrida (1930–2004), and to the deconstruction movement associated with his name. Derrida was a French philosopher whose most significant impact was in how words work, and the philosophical underpinnings of how words work. Deconstructionism, a so-called postmodern enterprise, is simply a particular manifestation of modernism, I believe. We might consider deconstructionism modernism with a vengeance applied to language. But it is more than a theory of language. There are issues of ultimate importance—of who God is, who man is, what creation is, what history is, and so on. Therefore, having an acquaintance with the thought of Derrida, and deconstructionism more generally, will serve as the backdrop against which to think through what the Christian faith has to say about the nature, meaning, and purpose of language.[28]

---

[28]Some Christians have less concern with deconstructionism as a dangerous ideology than I do. I particularly have in mind the work of James K. A. Smith, who has written several works from a different perspective than mine. See *The Fall of Language: Philosophical Foundations for a Creational Hermeneutic* (Downers Grove, IL: InterVarsity, 2000); *Jacques Derrida:*

THE GOSPEL AND THE MIND

The nature of language is central to postmodernism.[29] There is no one postmodern theory on words, language, and signs.[30] Indeed, the whole field of postmodern discussion, like most academic disciplines, consists of its own internal debates and developments.[31] Ludwig Wittgenstein (1889–1951) argued that language functions as a "language game," primarily valid within its own spheres.[32] Ferdinand de Saussure (1857–1913) argued that there is no inherent relationship between a word (the signifier—such as the word *cat*) and a thing (the signified—the furry animal).[33] Such relationships arise from custom and repetition.[34] Thus, Saussure wrote, "Language is a system of interdependent terms in which the value of each term results solely from the simultaneous presence of the others."[35] Indeed, "no one disputes the principle of the arbitrary nature of the sign."[36]

Live Theory (London: Continuum, 2005); *Who's Afraid of Postmodernism: Taking Derrida, Lyotard, and Foucault to Church* (Grand Rapids: Baker, 2006); *The Devil Reads Derrida: And Other Essays on the University, the Church, Politics, and the Arts* (Grand Rapids: Eerdmans, 2009). I have no personal animus toward Smith; I simply think deconstructionism is more harmful and more fundamentally anti-Christian than he does.
[29]In this section and in the rest of this chapter I will generally speak of postmodernity and deconstruction interchangeably.
[30]While some would balk at speaking of a postmodern *theory* of anything, the term is used here for convenience.
[31]For a helpful introduction to these issues, see James Wm. McClendon Jr. and James M. Smith, *Convictions: Defusing Religious Relativism*, rev. ed. (Valley Forge, PA: Trinity Press International, 1994), 19–45. See also Roger Lundin, *The Culture of Interpretation: Christian Faith and the Postmodern World* (Grand Rapids: Eerdmans, 1993), 185–211.
[32]McClendon and Smith, *Convictions*, 21–27. Anthony Thiselton suggests, contra Richard Rorty, that Wittgenstein did not hold to radically autonomous "language games." Rather, "the common behavior of humankind" (Wittgenstein's terminology) provides the "backing" for the meaning of language. Anthony Thiselton, *Interpreting God and the Postmodern Self: On Meaning, Manipulation, and Promise* (Grand Rapids: Eerdmans, 1995); Ludwig Wittgenstein, *Philosophical Investigations* (Oxford: Blackwell, 1967), sec. 54; Richard Rorty, *Philosophy and the Mirror of Nature* (Princeton: Princeton University Press, 1979), 356.
[33]Cf. the helpful book by Terry Eagleton, *Literary Theory: An Introduction*, 2nd ed. (Minneapolis: University of Minnesota Press, 1996), 84–85.
[34]McClendon and Smith, *Convictions*, 28–31; Lundin, *The Culture of Interpretation*, 187–89.
[35]Ferdinand de Saussure, *Course in General Linguistics*, trans. Charles Bally and Albert Sechehaye, in collaboration with Albert Reidlinger (London: Peter Owen, 1974), 114.
[36]Ibid., 68.

Particularly important as we move to Derrida, Saussure held that the meaning of a sign is constituted by its difference from other signs in its linguistic system. There is nothing inherent about *this* word (e.g., *hot*) referring to *that* thing (e.g., water).[37] Saussure bracketed the question of the actual "thing" outside the linguistic system, instead emphasizing the linguistic system itself. The structuralists continued Saussure's program and argued that texts (and many other things—e.g., societies) are composed of various structures—particularly opposites (e.g., hot/cold, male/female). As Terry Eagleton notes, "Structuralism in general is an attempt to apply [Saussure's] theory to objects and activities other than language itself."[38]

Most significant for our purposes is the movement that followed structuralism: deconstruction.[39] It is with deconstruction and its chief spokesman, Derrida, that one sees the most thoroughgoing rejection of any sort of "center" to words, language, and signs.[40]

---

[37]McClendon and Smith, *Convictions*, 29.

[38]Eagleton, *Literary Theory*, 84. Similarly, Frederic Jameson notes that structuralism is an attempt "to rethink everything through once again in terms of linguistics." See Jameson, *The Prison-House of Language: A Critical Account of Structuralism and Russian New Formalism* (Princeton: Princeton University Press, 1972), vii, quoted in Eagleton, *Literary Theory*, 84.

[39]I am treating deconstruction as an aspect of poststructuralism. We cannot go into detail here, but it is important to keep in mind the connection between Saussure/structuralism and deconstruction. As Eagleton notes (*Literary Theory*, 86), "Saussure's stress on the arbitrary relation between sign and referent, word and thing, helped to detach the text from its surrounding and make of it an autonomous object." Eagleton (*Literary Theory*, 111) summarizes the distinction between structuralism and poststructuralism as follows: "If structuralism divided the sign from the referent, this kind of thinking—often known as 'post-structuralism'—goes a step further: it divides the signifier from the signified." Diogenes Allen, "Christianity and the Creed of Postmodernism," *Christian Scholar's Review* 23 (December 1993): 122, likewise notes: "Deconstructionism, however, shares with structuralism the notion that meaning is intra-linguistic. It too is firmly anti-realist. Meaning is still a function of a system, *but in deconstructionism there is no universal system*" (emphasis mine).

[40]It is worth noting that Derrida can be terribly difficult to understand. Interviews of Derrida are sometimes the most cogent and understandable. See Richard Kearney, "Dialogue with Jacques Derrida," in *Dialogues With Contemporary Continental Thinkers: The Phenomenological Heritage* (Manchester: Manchester University Press, 1984), 105–26. Kearney's chapter on Derrida in his *Modern Movements in European Philosophy* (Manchester: Manchester University Press, 1987), 113–33, is also very helpful. For a critique of Derrida's attack on "presence" (which is an attack on Western metaphysics) see Brendan Sweetman, "The Deconstruction

Derrida's views on words and signs do not develop in a vacuum. They are related to his larger critique of Western metaphysics. Derrida posits that traditional Western metaphysics has privileged *speech* (the spoken word) over *writing* (the written word). This speech/writing dualism is due to a simple yearning for "full presence," which appears to mean something like "full and unveiled presence of one thing to another." Derrida explains, "The priority of spoken language over written or silent language stems from the fact that when words are spoken the speaker and the listener are supposed to be simultaneously present to one another; they are supposed to be the same, pure unmediated presence."[41] Derrida does not want simply to reverse the hierarchy, say, by privileging *writing* over *speech* (although ultimately writing is privileged or emphasized in his thought). Rather, he ultimately wishes to craft a new view of writing, a "writing" that encompasses both speech and (traditional) writing.[42]

Put another way, Derrida believes that the same issues that hound the written word also hound the spoken word. Both the written word and the spoken word consist of signs that point to other signs: "The secondarity that it seemed possible to ascribe to writing alone affects all signifieds in general, affects them always already, the moment they *enter the game*. There is not a single signified that escapes, even if recaptured, the play of signifying references that constitute

---

of Western Metaphysics: Derrida and Maritain on Identity," in *Postmodernism and Christian Philosophy*, ed. Roman T. Ciapolo (Mishawaka, IN: American Maritain Association; Washington, DC: The Catholic University of American Press, 1997), 230–47. Cf. Brian Ingraffia, *Postmodern Theory and Biblical Theology: Vanquishing God's Shadow* (Cambridge: Cambridge University Press, 1995), 167–224.

[41] In Kearney, *Dialogues With Contemporary Continental Thinkers*, 115. Cf. Derrida, *Of Grammatology* (Baltimore: Johns Hopkins University Press, 1998), 10–18.

[42] Derrida, *Of Grammatology*, 8–9, can speak of his view of writing as one which "exceeds and comprehends that of language." He also notes that "writing" includes "all that gives to the inscription in general, whether it is literal or not."

language."[43] Derrida argues that signs always *differ* from and *defer* to other signs in an endless "play" of signification—and this is the case with both speech and writing. This differing and deferring are the twin components of *différance*, a word coined by Derrida as a pun or game itself. A hybrid of *differ* and *defer*, *différance* is pronounced the same way as the French word *différence* would be, and thus the two are noticeably distinct only in writing.

In short, written texts consist of words, which point to words, which point to words, and there is no end to this "play" of pointing or signification. And while traditional metaphysics, according to Derrida, privileged the spoken word as somehow immune to or above this endless play, Derrida posits that both writing and speech are made up of signs that constantly point to other signs, with no end in sight and no determinate meaning to be attained.

Derrida's view on language is rooted in his own metaphysic. Writing ultimately precedes speech, and ultimately there is no experience of "presence" apart from language. This priority of writing entails several significant conclusions. First, signs are utterly central to all of life, and signs *precede* meaning. "We think only in signs," Derrida asserts.[44] But, if signs precede meaning, and if signs are exclusively defined in relation to other signs, and if these signs are engaged in an "endless signification," which consists of no origin and no telos, then ultimately meaning is never found. In Derrida's words, the "search for presence and fulfilment . . . is interminably deferred."[45]

---

[43]Ibid., 7. *Signified* simply means, in this context, "that which a sign points to."
[44]Ibid., 50. For a critique of the notion that we think in signs (or *only* in signs), see the work of Dallas Willard. Many of his essays are available at his Web site, dallaswillard.com.
[45]In Kearney, *Dialogues With Contemporary Continental Thinkers*, 126. Eagleton, *Literary Theory*, 112, summarizes this position: "Nothing is ever fully present in signs: it is an illusion for me to believe that I can ever be fully present to you in what I say or write, because to use signs

With his seminal essay, "Structure, Sign and Play in the Discourse of the Human Sciences," Derrida pointedly attacks any sort of metaphysical basis or foundation for words, language, and signs.[46] Particularly significant as we prepare to look at Augustine in the next chapter is Derrida's denial of "logocentrism." This denial runs throughout Derrida's work, but, surprisingly, it can be difficult to understand what Derrida means by this term. At times "logocentrism" simply denotes the privileged position speech has had over writing in Derrida's understanding of Western metaphysics. The *logos* of "logocentrism" is the spoken word, and logocentrism is the idea that in the spoken word there is the full presence of meaning.[47] But at other times the *logos* of "logocentrism" denotes broader concepts such as reason, the divine word, and even God's mind. G. C. Spivak, in the introduction to Derrida's *Of Grammatology*, writes that logocentrism is "the belief that the first and last things are the Logos, the Word, the Divine Mind, the infinite understanding of God, an infinitely creative subjectivity, and, closer to our time, the self-presence of full self-consciousness."[48] In Derrida's

---

at all entails that my meaning is always somehow dispersed, divided and never quite at one with itself."

[46]Jacques Derrida, "Structure, Sign and Play in the Discourse of Human Sciences," in *Writing and Difference*, trans. Alan Bass (Chicago: University of Chicago Press, 1978), 278–93. This essay was originally given at a symposium entitled, "The Languages of Criticism and the Sciences of Man," at Johns Hopkins University in October 1966. Roger Lundin notes that this lecture "proved to be a deadly opening salvo in the Continental invasion of American universities." See Lundin, *The Culture of Interpretation*, 189.

[47]Derrida, *Of Grammatology*, 43.

[48]G. C. Spivak, "Translator's Preface," in Derrida, *Of Grammatology*, lxviii. Likewise, Vincent Leitch, *Deconstructive Criticism* (New York: Columbia University Press, 1983), 24–25, notes that with Derrida "the logocentric system always assigns the origin of truth to the logos—to the spoken word, to the voice of reason, or to the Word of God" (quoted in John M. Ellis, *Against Deconstruction* [Princeton: Princeton University Press, 1989], 31). See Ellis's volume (esp. 30–44), for an excellent discussion and critique of Derrida's notion of logocentrism. Ellis concludes that ultimately the Derridean notion of logocentrism "is not a fixation on words, as one might expect, but instead a belief that there is an order of meaning existing *independently* of the structure of any given language that is a foundation for all else." Ellis holds that "logocentrism here turns out to be much the same as the more familiar *essentialism*, the belief that words simply label real categories of meaning existing independently of a language" (35).

own words, "That the logos is first imprinted and that that imprint is the writing-resource of language, signifies, to be sure, that the logos is not a creative activity, the continuous full element of the divine word, etc."[49]

Derrida specifically wishes to reject the *logos* (word) in favor of the "trace." He writes emphatically, "*The trace is in fact the absolute origin of sense in general. Which amounts to saying once again that there is no absolute origin of sense in general.*"[50] As Richard Kearney comments, "The text becomes an autonomous chain of signifiers irreducible to any fixed reference (transcendental signified) or intention (transcendental signifier) outside of the text. The deconstructed text is without origin or end."[51] According to Derrida, Levi-Strauss's "saddened, *negative*, nostalgic" and "guilty" yearning for "structure" is really a yearning for presence, which is the disruption of Derrida's notion of play.[52]

Derrida is quite clear that his option entails the rejection of any sort of normative meaning in words, language, and signs. His option entails "absolute chance," "genetic indetermination," and "the seminal adventure of the trace." It also entails the rejection of "full presence," of "the reassuring foundation," and (particularly significant for our study) of "the origin and end of play."[53] In short, there is no *origin* of words, language, and signs, and there is no *destination* or *eschatological goal* of words, language, and signs.

---

[49]Derrida, *Of Grammatology*, 68. Derrida notes (14–15) that with logocentrism the text as "fabric of signs" is "preceded by a truth, or a meaning already constituted by and within the element of the logos. Even when the thing, the 'referent,' is not immediately related to the logos of a creator God where it began by being the spoken/thought sense, the signified has at any rate an immediate relationship with the logos in general (finite or infinite), and a mediated one with the signifier, that is to say, with the exteriority of writing."

[50]Derrida, *Of Grammatology*, 65. Emphasis his.

[51]Kearney, *Modern Movements in European Philosophy*, 123.

[52]Derrida, "Structure, Sign and Play," 291–93.

[53]Ibid.

121

For Derrida, anything like a grounding of language in a larger Christian theological framework is explicitly rejected. There is no "transcendental signified" or "transcendental signifier," the logos is rejected in favor of the "trace," and interpretation is an endless play without origin or goal. If Derrida were correct, it would not bode well for Christian orthodoxy, but neither would it bode well for any meaningful use of language. Indeed, for Derrida's program to be correct, it must somehow be exempt from the deconstruction to which he subjects all other metaphysics.

Conclusion

Christianity is a religion of the book, and Christians are preeminently a people of the book, and hence a people of words.[54] Two of the most helpful resources for wrestling with the issues of language and communication are Augustine and, of course, Holy Scripture itself. For it is in Scripture and in the Christian tradition shaped by it (particularly Augustine) that we discover a way of thinking about words that can truly speak to contemporary challenges.

---

[54]For the most recent and thorough treatment of the constellation of issues related to being a "people of the book," see Jeffrey, *People of the Book.* Cf. Daniel E. Ritchie, *Reconstructing Literature in an Ideological Age: A Biblical Poetics and Literary Studies from Milton to Burke* (Grand Rapids: Eerdmans, 1996).

Thus in a certain fashion our word becomes a bodily sound by assuming that in which it is manifested to the senses of men, just as the Word of God became flesh by assuming that in which it too could be manifested to the senses of men.

AUGUSTINE

Allegory, in some sense, belongs not to medieval man but to man, or even to mind, in general. It is of the very nature of thought and language to represent what is immaterial in picturable terms.

C. S. LEWIS

It is not so much that the way language works helps us to understand the theology of the Incarnation, but rather that the theology of the Incarnation helps us profoundly to understand the way in which language works.

DAVID LYLE JEFFREY

The issue is, quite simply, that of the meaning of meaning as it is re-insured by the postulate of the existence of God.

GEORGE STEINER

5

Toward a Christian Understanding of Words

In the previous chapter I sketched some of the contemporary challenges related to language, giving particular attention to Jacques Derrida and deconstructionism. Derrida and deconstruction are representative of the contemporary mood. At the same time, my response in this chapter will range beyond the world of deconstruction as I outline a Christian understanding of language. We begin by considering what the doctrine of God tells us about the nature, importance, and purpose of words.

The God Who Speaks, Creates, and Rules

God himself is a speaking and communicating God. He created by words (Gen. 1:3ff.). He redeems by his Word— both Christ himself, the Word incarnate, and the inspired word/message of redemption in Christ. Jesus is the Word sent from heaven (John 1:1), and it is through the preaching of the gospel message that the power of God is unleashed (Rom. 1:16–17; 1 Cor. 1:18; 15:1–4; 2 Cor. 4:1–6). God blesses and renders judgment through words. Christians eagerly hope one day to hear their Master's words, "Well done, good and faithful servant" (Matt. 25:21, 23).

With all due respect to Augustine, to whom we will return shortly, language is not something that began with the fall. Consider God's communication described in John 16:13: "When the Spirit of truth comes, he will guide you into all the truth, for he will not speak on his own authority, but whatever he hears he will speak, and he will declare to you the things that are to come." Jesus tells us that the Holy Spirit *speaks* what he *hears* from the Father. There is no reason to think this speaking and hearing are rooted in sin. In fact, we have reason to believe that the members of the Trinity were speaking to one another before and apart from the entrance of sin into the world.[1]

If the Trinitarian God is truly a speaking God, and we are made in his image, it follows that *our* speech in some way reflects this Trinitarian character of God. That is, language is not simply a human artifice. Language is foremost a gift from God whereby we image or reflect God in the world. Although language is *utilized* by humanity, it has its origin in God. And thus we should be open to seeing analogies between God as the first and primary speaker and us as his image bearers who also use language. As Vern Poythress has written, "Relations of signification within language derive

---

[1]On the issue of language in Scripture, see the first chapter in Vern Sheridan Poythress, *In the Beginning Was the Word: Language—A God-Centered Approach* (Wheaton, IL: Crossway, 2009).

from the final relation of signification among the persons of the Trinity."[2]

Creation

Central to the Christian faith is the confession, "I believe in God, the Father Almighty, maker of heaven and earth." We live in a created order, and as one wrestles with the reality of language and words, it is hard to escape the importance of that truth. Why is creation so important? We find an answer in an older—and often overlooked—work by C. S. Lewis, *The Personal Heresy*, in which he debates with coauthor E. M. Tillyard.

Lewis argues that allegory helps constitute, in a sense, what it means to be human: "Allegory, in some sense, belongs not to medieval man but to man, or even to mind, in general. It is of the very nature of thought and language to represent what is immaterial in picturable terms."[3] Lewis turns to the twelfth-century Hugh of St. Victor to illustrate: "For Hugo, the material element in the Christian ritual is no mere concession to our sensuous weakness and has nothing arbitrary about it."[4] There is a "pre-existing *similitude* between the material element and the spiritual reality."

This is a fascinating notion, and if true, it is a robust denial of much of what passes for linguistic wisdom today. Lewis is suggesting that words are not simply human constructs haphazardly attached to this or that reality. On the contrary, there is a structure to reality such that there is a real and true relationship or connection between a material element and a spiritual reality. Lewis offers water and baptism as an example: "Water, *ex naturali qualitate*, was an image

---

[2] Poythress, *In the Beginning Was the Word*, 376.
[3] C. S. Lewis, *The Allegory of Love* (New York: Oxford University Press, 1958), 44.
[4] "Hugo" is a variant for the now more common "Hugh."

of the grace of the Holy Ghost even before the sacrament of baptism was ordained."[5]

What Lewis is saying astounds our contemporary ears. It is not the case that John the Baptist or Jesus chose arbitrarily to use water as a symbol of cleansing or forgiveness. It is not even that God foreknew from all eternity that water would in some way symbolize cleansing or forgiveness. Rather, Lewis is suggesting that in the very structure of things, in the very design of reality, there is a real and inextricable "similitude" (i.e., relationship, connection) between the water of baptism and the grace of the Holy Spirit. While Lewis does not delineate this theologically (at one level), it is worth reflecting on his point. For his argument to hold, it seems to need the kind of doctrine of creation outlined in this book. That is, if there is a genuine similitude between water and forgiveness of sins, then it seems that this relationship is embedded in the very structure of reality, the structure of the created order. And to put it in those terms is to move into the realm of the doctrine of creation.

When Lewis avers that some words are more *fitting* than others in reference to the created order, he is echoing Augustine's suggestion that God has structured the world in such a way that various aspects of creation might serve as "examples" for us. In his *Marriage and Desire*, Augustine writes:

> Divine providence has carefully provided certain trees which visibly exemplify these invisible realities which are incredible for those without faith, but are nonetheless true. After all, why should we not believe that this was the reason why he arranged it so that a wild olive is born of a domesticated one? Ought we not to believe that in something created for human use the

---

[5]Lewis, *The Allegory of Love*, 46.

creator provided and arranged what might serve as an example
of the human race? [6]

Colin Gunton makes a very similar argument in *The
Actuality of Atonement*. Gunton argues that the relationship
between a thing and the name of a thing is not necessarily a haphazard connection. Rather, because the world is
structured and created by God, the names of things—in a
sense—can fittingly and appropriately emerge over time
because there is a proper relationship between a thing and
its name. "Because the world is, so to speak, our shape and
we are world-shaped, there is a readiness of the world for
our language, a community of world and person which
enables the world to come to speech."[7] Following Richard
Boyd, Gunton suggests that "the world forces new mean-
ings upon words," and that language is "a subtle instrument
whose meaning is in part the gift of the (indwelt) world to
which it seeks to refer." Gunton continues, "The world gives
itself to be understood in the sense that its perceived and
experimentally revealed structures demand of us changes
in our language."[8]

In short, it just may be that the world, as a created
and structured reality, *shapes* and *influences* the words that
are generated to describe it. This does not mean that our
language always gets it right, but this view of the nature of
created reality helps us to realize that we live in an ordered
world, and that this world in some sense "calls out" for proper
language about itself.

---

[6]Augustine *Marriage and Desire* 19.21 (The Works of Saint Augustine: A Translation for the
21st Century, trans. Roland J. Teske, ed. John E. Rotelle [Hyde Park, NY: New City, 1998],
1:24).
[7]Colin Gunton, *The Actuality of the Atonement* (Edinburgh: T&T Clark, 1988), 38.
[8]Ibid., 48. Cf. Richard Boyd, "Metaphor and Theory Change: What Is a 'Metaphor' a Metaphor for?" in *Metaphor and Thought*, ed. A. Ortony (Cambridge: Cambridge University Press,
1979), 356–408.

A similar argument has been made by Geerhardus Vos (1862–1949). Vos held that when Jesus spoke in parables, he was not willy-nilly casting around for illustrations.

> It would be wrong to assume that the parables which Jesus spoke were nothing more than homiletical inventions, not based on any deeper principle or law. It would be more correct to call them spiritual discoveries, because they are based on a certain parallelism between the two strata of creation, the natural and the spiritual (redemptive) one, because the universe has been thus constructed.

All Jesus had to do "was to call attention to what had been lying hidden, more or less, since the time of creation."[9]

At the end of the first essay in *The Personal Heresy*, Lewis suggests that modern man faces a decision: either we are creatures who participate in a designed and meaningful universe, or we are not. If we do participate in a designed and meaningful universe, then our poetry can have meaning, and if we do not live in such a universe, our poetry cannot have meaning. The typical modern, as Lewis sees it, is a "half-hearted materialist" who essentially believes in a materialist and meaningless universe, but who (irrationally) asserts that what goes on in our heads has meaning.

> He [the typical modernist] thinks that everything except the buzzing electrons is a subjective fancy; and he therefore believes that all poetry must come out of the poet's head and express (of course) his pure, uncontaminated, undivided "personality," because outside the poet's head there is nothing but the interplay of blind forces.[10]

---

[9]Geerhardus Vos, *Biblical Theology: Old and New Testaments* (Grand Rapids: Eerdmans, 1948), 380. I first discovered this reference a number of years ago in the very helpful book by Moisés Silva, *God, Language and Scripture: Reading the Bible in the Light of General Linguistics* (Grand Rapids: Zondervan, 1990), 23.
[10]C. S. Lewis and E. M. W. Tillyard, *The Personal Heresy: A Controversy*, ed. Joel D. Heck (1939; Austin, TX: Concordia University Press, 2008), 28.

Lewis continues:

> Surely the dilemma is plain. Either there is significance in the whole process of things as well as in human activity, or there is no significance in human activity itself. It is an idle dream, at once cowardly and arrogant, that we can withdraw the human soul, as a mere epiphenomenon, from a universe of idiotic force, and yet hope, after that, to find for her some *faubourg* where she can keep a mock court in exile.[11]

In his final essay in *The Personal Heresy,* Lewis outlines the difference between his position and Professor Tillyard's. In doing so, Lewis gives attention—somewhat indirectly— to the goodness of creation and therefore to the splendor of commonplace, earthy things. Lewis writes of rains and sunsets:

> They respond, like chords of music, to some want within, unnoticed till the moment of its fulfillment. They fit the senses and imagination like an old glove. Momentary as they are, they seem (I hardly know how to say it) to have been prepared from all eternity for their precise place in the symphony of things— to be parts of a score rather than cross-sections of a process. . . . One of my chief grievances against the Personal Heresy and its inevitable attendant Poetolatry, is that disparagement of common things and common men which they induce.[12]

Efforts to understand language inevitably come up against the idea of creation. Christians should not be surprised by this. We live in God's world, his universe. As we created beings try to think about words and communication, it makes sense that we keep coming into contact with a created order. As chapter 1 has noted, if we do *not* live

---

[11]Ibid., 29.
[12]Ibid., 96.

in a created universe, it is impossible to account for the meaningfulness of the intellectual life. To justify any sort of affirmation of the meaningfulness of language, we need to affirm that we really do live in God's created world.

Why the Incarnation Matters

At the heart of the Christian faith is belief in the incarnation—the conviction that the eternal Son, the second member of the Trinity, a divine person, took on full humanity for our redemption. Without this confession there is no true Christianity. But why does it matter in a discussion of words?

Augustine wrote at length on the nature of language and words, and can help us navigate this terrain. Indeed, Umberto Eco's book on the nature of signs (the technical term is *semiotics*), moves from Plato all the way to Augustine as the first Christian thinker to deal with the reality of signs in a meaningful way.[13]

In his classic work *On Christian Doctrine* (written around AD 396), Augustine seeks to help teachers and preachers know how to interpret Scripture and communicate it to others. To do this, he takes up the relationship between signs and things.[14]

Book 1 deals mainly with things but also introduces signs. Augustine says, "All teaching is either about things

---

[13]See Umberto Eco, *Semiotics and the Philosophy of Language* (London: Macmillan, 1984).
[14]This section is simply a summary. There are places in *On Christian Doctrine* (*De doctrina Christiania*) where Augustine's treatment of signs will not concern this chapter. For example, in discussing the "proper" (i.e., plain or literal) and "metaphorical" senses of Scripture, Augustine uses the word *sign* (2.14; 2.23). This chapter does not broach, to any significant degree, such hermeneutical concerns. The two seminal articles on Augustine and signs are conveniently found reprinted in R. A. Markus, ed., *Augustine: A Collection of Critical Essays* (Garden City, NY: Anchor Books, 1972). See B. Darrell Jackson, "The Theory of Signs in St. Augustine's *De Doctrina Christiana*," 92–147; R. A. Markus, "St. Augustine on Signs," 61–91. Cf. Edmund Hill, "Sign and Language," introductory essay in *Teaching Christianity* (*De Doctrina Christiana*), The Works of Saint Augustine: A Translation for the 21st Century, ed. and trans. Edmund Hill (Hyde Park: New City, 1996), 28–53.

or signs" (1.2.2). Signs "are used to signify something else" (1.2.2). Signs are also things, because if signs were not also things, signs would be nothing. But this does not mean that every thing is a sign. In short, every sign is a thing, but not every thing is a sign.

I wonder if we could push Augustine here. Might we say, leaning on C. S. Lewis as quoted above, that all created reality is made up of signs—and these signs, each in its own unique way, proclaim something about the God who made them?

The triune God ("one supreme thing") is to be enjoyed, while all other things are to be used (1.5.5; 1.22.20). That is, all other things are to be used on one's journey to God (the "supreme thing").[15] Augustine affirms the limited nature of language: God is inexpressible. Yet even to say God is inexpressible is to say something about God (1.6.6). Augustine recognizes this dilemma and posits that God still "accepts" human words directed at him: God "has accepted the homage of human voices, and has wished us to rejoice in praising him with our words" (1.6.6). For Augustine, language can be "limited" but still be "useful" and adequate. This alone is a treasure worth plundering. Augustine offers a nuanced articulation of both the limited and the adequate nature of language.

In book 1 Augustine explicitly correlates words and the incarnate Word (1.13). The words we have in our minds are put into sounds (speech) that enter the ears of "flesh" of those to whom we wish to communicate. In a sense, our words become incarnate (in the flesh of ears), just as the

---

[15]David Lyle Jeffrey notes, "For Augustine even a theory of signs is therefore ultimately based on considerations of intention and the ordering of value." That is, Augustine's theory of signs is rooted in his ethical views, which are part of Augustine's larger Christian vision. See David Lyle Jeffrey, *People of the Book: Christian Identity and Literary Culture* (Grand Rapids: Eerdmans, 1996), 83.

preexistent Word (Christ) also became incarnate. And just as our word (thought) does not cease being a word when it becomes a sound, so God the Word did not cease to be the divine Word when the Word became incarnate in the man Jesus. Thus the incarnation of the Word provides an analogy for explaining the nature of our words.

Precisely at this point, Augustine offers something that may be constructive in the contemporary conversation regarding words, language, and signs.[16] Augustine is right to ground our words in *the* incarnate Word. Indeed, as David Lyle Jeffrey has written regarding Augustine, "It is not so much that the way language works helps us to understand the theology of the Incarnation, but rather that *the theology of the Incarnation helps us profoundly to understand the way in which language works.*"[17]

In book 2 of *On Christian Doctrine*, Augustine defines *sign*: "A sign, after all, is a thing, which besides the impression it conveys to the senses, also has the effect of making something else come to mind" (2.1.1). Signs can be natural or conventional (the latter concern Augustine more) (2.1.2). Natural signs are those whose signification is not due to human intent; for example, smoke is a sign of fire; an angry person expresses anger with a frown, even if unintentionally (2.11.2). Conventional signs are the result of the human intent to signify; for example, someone addresses someone else in words with the intention of communicating (2.2.3). The signs that mainly concern Augustine are words, although other signs are legitimate (2.3). This concern for words is

---

[16]Rowan Williams explicates many of these issues in "Language, Reality and Desire in Augustine's *De Doctrina,*" *Journal of Literature and Theology* 3, no. 2 (1989): 138–49. Williams notes that for Augustine, since God is the ultimate *res* (thing), and our desires are focused on God (or should be), signs in this life are to be simply used as one journeys to God (esp. 140). Cf. Werner G. Jeanrond, "Hermeneutics and Christian Praxis: Some Reflections on the History of Hermeneutics," *Journal of Literature and Theology* 2, no. 2 (1988): 180–82.
[17]Jeffrey, *People of the Book*, 83–84. Emphasis mine.

particularly tied to the words of Scripture, by which God communicates to his creatures (2.2.3).

In summary, Augustine offers a philosophy of signs that grounds our words in the incarnate Word and directs our signs (words) to the ultimate "thing," God. This gives our language an eschatological focus and meaning. Words, language, and signs, for Augustine, are inherently tied to the nature and purposes of God. We can draw from Augustine's formulation a doctrine of words, language, and signs in explicitly Christian theological terms.

In Augustine's *The Trinity* (written across the span of 399–419) he also takes up the issue of language and wrestles with the relationships between the preexistent Word, the incarnate Word, and our words. In a treatment of the Trinity, and hence Christ the Word, one is justified in asking whether Augustine also addresses the issues of words, language, and signs. We turn our attention to those places where Augustine explicitly deals with our topic.

Augustine expressly correlates our words and the incarnate Word (Christ). In 7.4 Augustine argues from the lesser to the greater: if our words are capable of declaring and accomplishing their purpose, how much more so for the divine Word, which was the agent of creation, and which became incarnate in the Son?

In 15.20 of *The Trinity*, Augustine makes almost the same argument as in *On Christian Doctrine* 1.13. In *The Trinity* he explicates the argument more thoroughly. A word uttered outwardly (aloud) begins as an internal word. Augustine compares such uttered words with the incarnation: "In a certain fashion our word becomes a bodily sound by assuming that in which it is manifested to the senses of men, just as the Word of God became flesh by assuming that in which it too could be manifested to the senses of men." He continues, "And just as our word becomes sound without being changed into sound, so the Word of God became flesh, but it is unthinkable that it should have been changed into flesh. It is by assuming it, not by being consumed into it, that both our word becomes sound and that Word became flesh" (15.20).

Augustine sees a "likeness" between our words and the Word of God, Christ (15.20). Augustine discusses how man is made in the image of God, which is pictured as an enigmatic mirror. A central part of this image is human rationality. Augustine argues that it is impossible to obtain an exhaustive intellectual understanding of the Trinity (15.6–13). Even though such an understanding is impossible, Augustine posits that in the mind there can be a type of word that is not even formulated or internally spoken. If we can think of this type of word, then we "can already see through this mirror and in this enigma some likeness of that Word of which it is said, *In the beginning was the Word, and the Word was with God, and the Word was God* (Jn. 1:1)" (15.19).[18] Augustine also correlates our works (which begins with words) with God's work of creation (brought about through the Word) (15.20). That is, just as the preexistent Word was the agent of creation (Phil. 2:6; Col. 1:16; Heb. 1:2–3), and thus God's Word originates his work, so our words (first in the mind and then spoken) originate our works.

Augustine concludes this section by offering one more correlation between our words and the Word, a correlation that explains why the Son, and not the other members of the Trinity, became incarnate. The eternal Son (the Word) became flesh that "we might live rightly by our word fol-

---

[18]It is this unformulated (nonlinguistic?) word that is the most puzzling as we attempt to learn from Augustine. If what is really important is this unspoken and unformulated word, what does this imply for the preexistent Word, the incarnate Word, and the written Word?

lowing and imitating his example; that is by having no false-hood either in the contemplation or in the operation of our word" (15.20). Thus, Christ was the obedient Word who became incarnate, and through his perfect example as the Word incarnate we are to execute our words in imitation of him.

The Trinity yields the mother lode of Augustine's thoughts on the relation between the incarnate Word and our words. At the same time, we see hints of Augustine's disposition for the unformulated, unspoken, interior, and even nonlinguistic word in *The Trinity*. The last is the most puzzling component, as it seems to diminish the very incarnation, an incarnation that provides some of the richest conceptions for understanding the nature of language.

Christ the Teacher

If we turn to Augustine's *The Teacher*, we find additional insights into the nature of words. In this small but important work, Augustine deals both with words and with the more general question of how we know anything at all.

Written in AD 389 (not long after Augustine's conversion in 386), *The Teacher* features his early thoughts on language and signs. It is a sustained dialogue between Augustine and his son Adeodatus dealing with words and understanding.

In 1.1–2 Augustine and Adeodatus agree that the purpose of speaking is to teach and to learn. In 2.3–4.7 they agree that often signs simply point to other signs and not to the signified thing itself.[19] Augustine is led to a threefold division: (1) certain signs can be pointed out with other

---

[19]However, two things can be pointed out without signs: (1) "things we aren't doing when we are asked [about them] and yet can do on the spot"; and (2) "the very signs we happen to be 'doing' [when asked about them], just as when we speak we are making signs (and [the word] 'signifying' is derived from this [activity])" (4.7).

signs; (2) things that are not signs can be also be pointed out by signs ("giving signs with which they may be brought to one's attention"); and (3) things that are not signs can be exhibited by doing them (e.g., walking) (4.7).[20]

An example of the first part of this classification (signs pointing to signs) would be the signs *name* and *word*. Both these terms (1) signify themselves, (2) are "mutually signified by the other," (3) are such that "whatever is signified by the one is also signified by the other," and (4) "differ from each other in nothing aside from sound" (6.18.47–51).

In the second part of Augustine's threefold classification (signs that signify things), Augustine posits that the thing signified is more important than the sign. That is, words are used for a reason—to bring concepts and things to mind: "Knowledge of things is more valuable than the signs of things."

We see in *The Teacher* that Augustine, some sixteen hundred years before our time, is dealing with the same issues that have been playing out in contemporary language theory. He prefigures Saussure in distinguishing between the sign and the signified, and although Saussure "brackets" the issue of external referent (the object itself), Augustine affirms that signs often do refer to things themselves (although Augustine holds that things are often signs as well). Perhaps most intriguing to our study is Augustine's conclusion. He argues that ultimately one learns nothing from signs. Unless one is already familiar with the thing signified, the sign will be a meaningless sound to the recipient of the sign. Augustine

---

[20]Augustine appears to be quite a few years ahead of his time in that he appears to emphasize that meaning is located at the level of sentences and beyond. Augustine asks Adeodatus to note what each word in the following sentence signifies: "If nothing from so great a city it pleases the gods be left . . ." Adeodatus quickly realizes the difficulty of such a task (2.1–20). Augustine's (unspoken) point would seem to be that meaning is best found in sentences and larger units.

writes, "We don't learn anything by these signs called words." Instead, "we learn the meaning of a word—that is, the signification hidden in the sound—once the thing signified is itself known, rather than our perceiving it by means of such signification" (10.34.155–59). In short, a word or sign can only make sense to us *after* we know the thing signified.

Is this a step toward despair or nihilism for Augustine? Not at all. Augustine's assertion that we learn nothing from signs leads to his discussion on the "inner Teacher," Christ. Augustine writes that when Christ teaches someone, this person is "taught not by my words but by the things themselves made manifest within when God discloses them" (12.40.38–39). Christ within the person must "enlighten" or "illumine" him, allowing him to learn.[21] People can have an "inner light of Truth," which results in illumination and rejoicing (12.40.31–33). To determine "whether truths have been stated," students look "upon the inner Truth" (14.45.5–10). The ultimate goal of teaching is "to be inwardly turned toward Him" (15.46.24–27).

To summarize, Augustine posits that it is Christ himself who illumines people, disclosing and revealing that they might know. Christ illumines the human mind, allowing people to learn—or better put, Christ *teaches* people himself. Here is a thoroughgoing *logos* doctrine. Not only does Christ give meaning to the universe and hence language, but Christ himself is the teacher. At the same time, the relation between words and the teacher is ambiguous at

---

[21]Augustine does not address the issue of the differences between Christians and non-Christians. Nor does he address the way in which Christ is "in" the Christian versus how Christ is "in" the non-Christian. Whereas biblically Christ lives in the believer (e.g., Col. 1:27), Scripture never speaks of Christ being "in" the non-Christian. This chapter will not discuss at length the issue of Augustine and illumination. On this issue see Ronald H. Nash, *The Light of Mind: St. Augustine's Theory of Knowledge* (Lexington, KY: University of Kentucky Press, 1969). For a short summary of Augustine's theory of illumination see Mary T. Clark, *Augustine*, Outstanding Christian Thinkers (London: Geoffrey Chapman, 1994), 19–25. Cf. Etienne Gilson, *The Christian Philosophy of Saint Augustine* (New York: Random House, 1960), 66–111.

points. Does the teacher illumine the mind to understand the words? Is the illumination *a*-linguistic? Augustine's apparent preference for a nonverbal illumination is the type of thing Derrida attacks. In Derrida's view, the spoken word has been privileged over the written word in traditional Western metaphysics because supposedly the spoken word involves a full presence lacking in the written word.

Words, Redemption, and Telos
One of the most important things we can glean from Augustine regarding words is his understanding of the theological context of language, and the ultimate redemptive and eschatological purpose of language. For Augustine, words are a part of God's good world and play a significant role in God's creation. Indeed, the nature of language and words can be fully and truly appreciated only when we see this world as God's world, and when we discover how words function as a part of God's plan.

Words have a soteriological, redemptive purpose. Remember, for Augustine there are signs and things. Words are signs that point to things, and things are either to be used or enjoyed.[22] The ultimate "thing" to be enjoyed is the triune God, who is *the* "Thing" (*res*).[23] Augustine's teaching, then, is that our words ultimately have a telos—the triune God. The telos to all communication is the vision and presence of God. All words are types of signs, or pointers, which find their culmination and goal in the God of Scripture.

The notion of an ultimate telos to all language is what, of course, is missing in the deconstructionist universe of Derrida. Whereas for Derrida there is no *logos* or "transcendental signified"—no ultimate reality as the goal or center

---

[22]Augustine *On Christian Doctrine* 1.3.
[23]Ibid., 1.5.

of language—for Augustine there certainly is. God himself is the goal of all language. While we often think of teleology in relation to Aristotle, the tendency to think in terms of ultimate goals and ends is central to Augustine.

Our use of language may have an intermediate goal—a goal at hand, such as communicating with a friend. But intermediate goals are best understood within the broader view of one's ultimate goal of loving, knowing, and glorifying God. When we come to see *all* communication as ultimately a part of the life of glorifying God, our words take on a grand significance. We come to understand the significance of passages like Ephesians 4:29, where Paul commands, "Let no corrupting talk come out of your mouths, but only such as is good for building up, as fits the occasion . . ." Note how Paul ends this command: ". . . that it may give grace to those who hear." Our words have the capacity to *give grace*, and thereby to glorify God within the larger landscape of his sovereign plan.

The Christian believes that words are instrumental in reaching out to fallen man. Words are not an end in themselves. They play a crucial role in leading people to the *res*, God. For the Christian, God is the "transcendental signified" to which all language ultimately points. In a world created with words, we use words on our journey to be conformed to *the* Word, Christ. This is in contradistinction to the "endless play" of Derrida's words pointing to words pointing to words. Augustine's position provides an *origin* and *destiny* to language (and all of life), both of which are missing in Derrida's "play." The origin of language is rooted in the triune God, and language is made particularly meaningful by the incarnate Word, the second member of the Trinity. Language also has an eschatological destiny as we participate in God's redemptive plan for the

THE GOSPEL AND THE MIND

universe. Thus, our language culminates in and points to the nature and work of God.

A Better "Logocentrism"

As Christians, we should certainly be *logos*-centered people, and Augustine helps us to formulate a more biblical and nuanced logocentrism. Whether we retain the term *logocentrism* is not particularly important.[24] What is important is the centrality of the divine Logos in relation to the realities of words, language, and signs. In the better logocentrism offered by Augustine and historic Christianity, *logos* denotes not only the spoken word, but also the written word, and preeminently Christ himself: preexistent, incarnate, resurrected, and now interceding for the saints.

Christianity has a *lower* or more reticent view of speech than that outlined in Derrida's "traditional Western metaphysic." Traditional Christianity is well aware that our use of language, after the fall, is fraught with difficulty, misperception, misunderstanding, the need to say things again and again, and so on. Traditional Christianity is not naive or utopian about our contemporary use of language. Christians do not affirm that with the spoken word we have a full, absolute presence of meaning.[25]

At the same time, traditional Christianity has a *higher* view of writing than the one targeted by Derrida's critique of Western metaphysics. Being a word-centered people, Christians know that the written word can (to a significant degree) be understood in meaningful, effective communi-

---

[24]Jeffrey, *People of the Book*, 10, correctly notes that deconstructionists associate Christianity with a confused definition of logocentrism. Jeffrey concludes, "Christian theory may be Logos-centered, but it is not logocentrism" (as defined by Derrida).

[25]In ibid., 16, Jeffrey notes: "The perennial generation of words . . . is not a function of either the dearth or the plenitude of their meaning. It is a function rather of our getting it at best about half-right, because language, even when communicating the divine Word, is simultaneously both revelatory and distorting."

cation. So we may affirm, with George Steiner, that there is a *"real* presence," rather than a *"full* presence." He states, "The meaning of meaning . . . is re-insured by the postulate of the existence of God."[26]

The Possibility of Repentance

In the last chapter of his *The People of the Book*, David Lyle Jeffrey argues that the eclipse of certain narratives (by strands of critical theory) renders it difficult for such critical theory to accurately deal with texts concerning ethics or virtue.[27] The narratives Jeffrey has in view are "narratives of repentance" such as Augustine's *Confessions*, Dostoevsky's *Crime and Punishment*, and Isaac Bashevis Singer's *The Penitent*.

Jeffrey's quotation from Kierkegaard is strikingly apropos in relationship to the present age. Kierkegaard is suggesting that certain phony revolutionaries do not tear down everything in sight, but leave things standing while emptying all things of significance:

> A passionate and tumultuous age will overthrow everything, pull everything down; but a revolutionary age, that is at the same time reflective and passionless, transforms that expression of strength into a feat of dialectics; it leaves everything standing but cunningly empties it of significance. Instead of culminating in a rebellion it reduces the inward reality of all relationships to a reflective tension which leaves everything standing but leaves the whole of life ambiguous: so that everything continues to exist factually whilst by a dialectical deceit, *privatissime*, it supplies a *secret interpretation*—that it does not exist.[28]

What Jeffrey is arguing is truly fascinating. "Narratives of repentance" are designed by their authors to elicit a

---

[26]George Steiner, *Real Presences* (Chicago: University of Chicago Press, 1989), 120.
[27]Jeffrey, *People of the Book*, 357.
[28]Ibid., 358.

THE GOSPEL AND THE MIND

repentant response in the reader. Perhaps the clearest examples are certain parables, such as the parable of the Pharisee and the tax collector. In this parable the Pharisee prays, in effect, "Lord, thank you that I am not like those poor miserable sinners over there." The tax collector on the other hand prays, with head bent, "God, be merciful to me, a sinner!" (Luke 18:13). The tax collector goes home justified, not the Pharisee. Such a parable clearly portrays repentance and implicitly calls the reader to repentance as well.

Much of the world of critical theory would preclude such a "straightforward" or "realistic" reading. For critical theory, particularly of the deconstructionist kind, such a plain reading would be ruled out of bounds from the beginning. But here is an example of how the Christian understanding of God, man, and the world encourages the intellectual life by allowing a proper reading of such a narrative. If a theory disallows the obviously intended reading from the beginning, then someone who holds to such a view is barred from a proper understanding of "narratives of repentance" from the start. In a Christian understanding of the world, where words are often used for correction and rebuke, it makes sense that some stories have been generated to induce repentance. But if one's ultimate understanding of reality (including words and texts) disqualifies a reading that allows words to function in a repentance-inducing way, then one will be hindered from relating to such texts aright.

Conclusion

Walker Percy suggests that it is ultimately the Christian vision of the world that can account for the reality of narrative, and indeed of the novel. "There is a special kinship between the novel as an art form and Christianity as an

ethos. . . . It is no accident, I think, that the novel is a creature of the Christian West and is virtually nonexistent in
the Buddhist, Taoist, and Brahmin East, to say nothing of
Marxist countries." Percy writes further:

> Though most current novelists may not be believing Christians
> or Jews, they are still living in a Judeo-Christian ethos. If, in fact,
> they are living on the fat of the faith, so to speak, one can't help
> but wonder what happens when the fat is consumed. Perhaps
> there are already signs. Witness the current loss of narrative of
> character and events in the post-modern novel.

Percy continues:

> It is no accident that the novel has never flourished in the
> Eastern tradition. If Buddhism and Hinduism believe that the
> self is illusory, that ordinary life is misery, that ordinary things
> have no sacramental value, and that reality itself is concealed
> by the veil of *maya*, how can any importance be attached to
> or any pleasure be taken in novels about selves and happen-
> ings and things in an ordinary world?[29]

George Steiner reflects on the break between word and
world in modernism:

> It is my belief that this contract is broken for the first time,
> in any thorough and consequent sense, in European, Central
> European and Russian culture and speculative consciousness
> during the decades from the 1870s to the 1930s. *It is this break
> of the covenant between word and world which constitutes one
> of the very few revolutions of spirit in Western history and which
> defines modernity itself.*[30]

---

[29]Walker Percy, *Signposts in a Strange Land* (New York: Farrar, Straus and Giroux, 1991),
365–66.
[30]Steiner, *Real Presences*, 112. Emphasis mine.

If Christians can learn one key thing from Derrida and deconstructionism, it might be the following: *we should always think in radically Christian ways and categories about all of reality*, and *apart from the realities of creation, fall, redemption, and consummation it is impossible to hold to a view of the meaningfulness of language.* Indeed, we should not think of language as neutral, something simply *there* that we must invent a way to think about Christianly. Rather, we should recognize language as a gift of God, given for his purposes, to be used on his terms. And we should confess that Christ is Lord of language, and that any proper recovery of a meaningful understanding of words and language in our day will be an understanding that is fundamentally and inextricably theological and Christ-centered. For that is the only way—at the end of the day—to truly understand any part of God's good world.

It is clear that when we live according to God our mind should be intent on his invisible things and thus progressively be formed from his eternity, truth and charity. . . . For knowledge too is good within its own proper limits if what puffs up or tends to puff up in it is overcome by the love of eternal things, which does not puff up but builds up, as we know. Indeed without knowledge one cannot have the virtues which make for right living and by which this woeful life is so conducted that one may finally reach the truly happy life which is eternal.

AUGUSTINE

Our inability to know the truth is the consequence of our corruption, our moral decay.

FRIEDRICH NIETZSCHE,
SUMMARIZING THE VIEW OF BLAISE PASCAL

People try to persuade us that the objections against Christianity spring from doubt. The objections against Christianity spring from insubordination, the dislike of obedience, rebellion against all authority.

SØREN KIERKEGAARD

Our mind cannot apprehend God without rendering some honor to him.

JOHN CALVIN

6

The Moral Nature of Knowledge and the Human Heart

It is cliché to observe that the modern age has seen a veritable explosion of information. Given our pride, it is tempting to boast in our ability to quote this or that fact, or give the latest tidbit of information from an Internet news service. Sixty years ago, long before the Internet, Richard Weaver could speak of "the astonishing vogue of factual information."[1] And more than one commentator has written on the divorce of knowledge from moral action. Dorothy Sayers wrote, more than a generation ago, "It is worse than useless for Christians to talk about the importance of Christian morality, unless they are prepared to take their stand upon the fundamentals of Christian theology."[2]

---

[1]Richard Weaver, *Ideas Have Consequences* (Chicago: University of Chicago Press, 1948), 58.
[2]Dorothy Sayers, *Creed or Chaos* (Manchester, NH: Sophia Institute Press, 1974), 31.

THE GOSPEL AND THE MIND

I have been teaching since I was in graduate school. As of this writing, I have taught for nearly twelve years in a college setting, almost entirely with undergraduates. I have consistently taught students who—at one level— simply wanted the "goods" they needed to know for the test. For a lot of reasons, including the kind of education most students in America currently receive, few students view learning as a grand adventure, as coming into contact with the "truth of things" (Aquinas), as part of the cultivation of wisdom, eloquence, and virtue, or as somehow intricately linked with their real lives—at least not their ethical lives. And it is that last emphasis—the moral nature of knowledge and the relationship between knowledge and action—that concerns me here.

To Know God Is to Honor Him

My thinking in this direction, to the best of my memory, was sparked partially by something I read in John Calvin's *Institutes*. It is well known that Calvin structures the *Institutes* around the theme of the knowledge of God. There is knowledge of the God the *Creator* (book 1) and knowledge of God the *Redeemer* (book 2). Calvin provocatively explores the relationship between the knowledge of the self and the knowledge of God, arguing for a type of symbiotic relationship between the two.

Of interest to me here is the *way* in which Calvin construes knowledge of God. Calvin contends—and the implications of this insight are fascinating—that to know God is to honor him. It is not that we know God, and then at some later point we may or may not act on that knowledge by honoring God. Rather, Calvin's point is that the honoring is included within the knowledge itself. Thus Calvin says,

"Our mind cannot apprehend God without rendering some honor to him."[3]

In chapter 3, we discussed at some length how an understanding of sin and redemption can inform a construal of the intellectual life. Sin does not simply color part of our lives; it colors all of who we are and all of what we do, including our intellectual endeavors. And so it is appropriate in this final chapter to think about the moral nature of knowledge and the relationship between knowledge and action.

I am going to challenge any hard and fast dichotomy between knowledge and action. I will follow Calvin in saying that to know God *is* to honor him. While Calvin is speaking specifically about the knowledge of God, I wonder whether we might extend his insight into knowledge more generally. Might it be helpful to think of knowledge as virtually always having a moral component? Does knowing something ultimately entail properly relating to what is known, and are such proper relations inherently a moral issue?

The late British theologian Colin Gunton was fond of the quotation, "Modernism began and continues wherever civilisation began and continues to *deny* Christ."[4] That is, modernism should be understood as more than simply a series of intellectual moves made in a certain time period (say, the 1600s, 1700s, or 1800s) by key figures (say, Descartes, Locke, Hume, Kant). We will look with greater focus at our own age (the modern or so-called postmodern age)

---

[3] John Calvin, *Institutes of the Christian Religion*, ed. John T. McNeill, trans. Ford Lewis Battles (Philadelphia: Westminster, 1960), 1.11.1.
[4] Colin E. Gunton, *The One, the Three and the Many: God, Creation and the Culture of Modernity.* The Bampton Lectures 1992 (Cambridge: Cambridge University Press, 1994), 1. Cf. Peter Fuller, *Theoria: Art and the Absence of Grace* (London: Chatto and Windus, 1988), 139. Gunton attributes this quotation to William Morris, but it appears actually to be from John Ruskin, *Lectures on Architecture and Painting* (New York: John Wiley and Son, 1865), 157.

shortly, and try to come to terms with it. But first we look
to Scripture to get a sense of the nature of knowledge.

Back to the Beginning
To begin thinking biblically about knowledge and its moral
implications, we need to go back to the beginning. In Genesis, when God creates the man and the woman, he commands them, "Be fruitful and multiply and fill the earth and
subdue it and have dominion over the fish of the sea and
over the birds of the heavens and over every living thing
that moves on the earth" (Gen. 1:28). In the second chapter of Genesis, God places man in a garden (Gen. 2:8) and
then gives him a command "to work it and keep it" (v. 15).
Then in verses 16–17 man is given a command with a consequence or sanction attached to it: "You may surely eat of
every tree of the garden, but of the tree of the knowledge
of good and evil you shall not eat, for in the day that you
eat of it you shall surely die." I simply note here that man's
existence from the beginning was morally structured and
ethically constituted. God provided for all of man's needs
and gave him commands and a prohibition. Human existence was at its core ethical and moral.

It is significant that in Genesis 3 the first thing the
Serpent says to the woman is, "Did God actually say, 'You
shall not eat of any tree in the garden'?" (v. 1). The Serpent initiates his conversation by questioning what God
has said. Eve responds by summarizing God's prohibition,
but—as more than one commentator notes—she apparently adds a prohibition, "Neither shall you touch it" (v. 3).
Is she already becoming confused simply by entering into
conversation with the Evil One?[5] The Serpent responds

[5]See the excellent work by Henri Blocher, *Original Sin: Illuminating the Riddle* (Leicester:
Apollos, 1997).

with a straightforward challenge to God's command, and hence to God himself: "You will not surely die" (v. 4). The woman—and the man—of course do transgress God's prohibition, and the rest of the chapter records the consequences of their sin.

This account testifies to the moral nature of the knowledge the first couple possessed. God created them, placed them in the garden, provided for them, and gave them commands and one prohibition. The first couple were morally culpable for what God had spoken. They were morally accountable for the knowledge they had received. Eve—the conversation partner in the opening lines of Genesis 3—had a moral decision to make about what she knew. She *knew* that God had spoken, and the Serpent initiated a discussion in which Eve had to decide whether she would live up to what she really knew. There appears to be no reason for her to have doubted what God had said. Yet, she disobeyed God, and Genesis mentions three things that contributed to her decision to disobey: the woman saw that the tree of the knowledge of good and evil was (1) good for food, (2) a delight to the eyes, and (3) desirable for making her wise. And so we are witnesses to a battle between what is known (God's prohibition) and misguided desires.

It is hard to know exactly what to make of the tree of the knowledge of good and evil. Somehow, at the heart of God's only prohibition is a limitation of knowledge. The first sin—and the most significant, in an obvious sense—was an exchange of proper knowledge for improper knowledge. Indeed, after the transgression, Genesis records that "the eyes of both were opened, and they knew that they were naked" (Gen. 3:7). The knowledge gained was knowledge that God did not want them to have (at least not yet).

As we look ahead in Scripture, we see a common emphasis on the moral nature of knowledge. In 1 Samuel 2:3, Hannah prays,

> Talk no more so very proudly,
>> let not arrogance come from your mouth;
> for the LORD is a God of knowledge,
>> and by him actions are weighed.

Because the Lord is a God of knowledge, he weighs actions—and we can be sure that he weighs them justly. The book of Job makes a similar connection, when Job asks,

> Will any teach God knowledge,
>> seeing that he judges those who are on high? (Job 21:22)

God's knowledge can be seen as the foundation of his just judgment.

Solomon, in praying to God for help in governing Israel, can speak of knowledge and wisdom in the same breath: "Give me now wisdom and knowledge to go out and come in before this people, for who can govern this people of yours, which is so great?" (2 Chron. 1:10). Knowledge is not simply a collection of facts; it is coupled with wisdom, and this coupling is repeated in verses 11 and 12.

The Psalms make a compelling link between a *lack* of knowledge and being *evil*, as the following verses demonstrate:

> Have they no knowledge, all the evildoers
>> who eat up my people as they eat bread
>> and do not call upon the LORD? (Ps. 14:4)

> They have neither knowledge nor understanding,
>> they walk about in darkness;
>> all the foundations of the earth are shaken. (Ps. 82:5)

> Have those who work evil no knowledge,
>> who eat up my people as they eat bread,
>> and do not call upon God? (Ps. 53:4)

Summarizing how God works in the lives of his people the psalmist links the Lord's *rebuke* with the fact that God gives knowledge:

> He who disciplines the nations, does he not rebuke?
> He who teaches man knowledge—
>> the LORD—knows the thoughts of man,
>> that they are but a breath. (Ps. 94:10–11)

The Lord who *disciplines* is the Lord who teaches man knowledge. This same connection is found in Proverbs 12:1:

> Whoever loves discipline loves knowledge,
>> but he who hates reproof is stupid.

Indeed, the love of discipline and the love of knowledge go together.

In Psalm 119 David connects *good judgment* with knowledge:

> Teach me good judgment and knowledge,
>> for I believe in your commandments. (Ps. 119:66)

Note that knowledge is tied to *good judgment* and a positive understanding of God's *commandments*.

A central passage in this whole discussion is Proverbs 1:7:

> The fear of the LORD is the beginning of knowledge;
>> fools despise wisdom and instruction.

This classic text has shaped Christian reflection, particularly the idea of "faith seeking understanding." The beginning of true knowledge requires the fear of the Lord. Learning is far from a morally neutral process. A similar teaching is found in Proverbs 9:10:

> The fear of the LORD is the beginning of wisdom,
>   and the knowledge of the Holy One is insight.

Perhaps often overlooked in Proverbs 1:7 is the last part. It is not only true that those who want knowledge must fear the Lord. So that no one misses the point, the proverb continues, "fools despise wisdom and instruction." Some people actually do not want wisdom or instruction. They would rather be fools than gain wisdom or heed instruction. Similarly, in Proverbs 1:22 we read that "fools hate knowledge." And Proverbs 1:29 speaks of consequences some would suffer,

> because they hated knowledge
>   and did not choose the fear of the LORD.

Other Proverbs sound the same theme regarding the moral nature of knowledge. For example,

> The heart of him who has understanding seeks knowledge,
>   but the mouths of fools feed on folly. (Prov. 15:14)

> An intelligent heart acquires knowledge,
>   and the ear of the wise seeks knowledge. (Prov. 18:15)

The prophets are replete with the same themes. Isaiah even says that the people of God have been taken into captivity because of a lack of knowledge:

> Therefore my people go into exile
>   for lack of knowledge. (Isa. 5:13)

Similarly, in Hosea we read,

> My people are destroyed for lack of knowledge;
> because you have rejected knowledge,
> I reject you from being a priest to me.
> And since you have forgotten the law of your God,
> I also will forget your children. (Hos. 4:6)

And when Nebuchadnezzar, the king of Babylon, was seeking good counsel and help, he sought persons who combined numerous qualities, including knowledge: "youths without blemish, of good appearance and skillful in all wisdom, endowed with knowledge, understanding learning, and competent to stand in the king's palace, and to teach them the literature and language of the Chaldeans" (Dan. 1:4).

In the New Testament, Jesus says, essentially, that to know him—savingly, intimately—means to obey his commandments. For example: "If you love me, you will keep my commandments" (John 14:15); and "Whoever has my commandments and keeps them, he it is who loves me" (v. 21). Similarly "If anyone loves me, he will keep my word" (v. 23). A slightly different emphasis is found in 1 John 2:3, where command keeping is *confirmation* that we know Jesus: "And by this we know that we have come to know him, if we keep his commandments." Indeed, in 1 John 5:3, keeping God's commands is virtually equated with loving him: "For this is the love of God, that we keep his commandments. And his commandments are not burdensome."

The apostle Paul often speaks of the importance of knowledge, including its moral nature. In a particularly provocative statement, he *warns* his readers about knowledge. In the context of addressing the issue of food offered to idols in Corinth, Paul writes that "'knowledge' puffs

157

up, but love builds up" (1 Cor. 8:1). He goes on to say, "If anyone imagines that he knows something, he does not yet know as he ought to know" (v. 2). On first reading this, we might be tempted to think that knowledge in general, or as a rule, "puffs up," and therefore we should avoid it. But upon closer look, and in light of what we have seen above, Paul is not discouraging knowledge itself. The fact that knowledge can puff up—and often does—illustrates the central point of this chapter: *knowledge is inherently a moral reality*—it will be used for good or ill. Paul's warning in verse 2 reinforces this point. He seems to be saying something like: "If you think that you have arrived intellectually, and that you *truly* grasp the heart of reality, you are showing that you do not in fact know in the way you ought to know." Thus, Paul is driving home the point that *the way we know* and *what we think about what we know* are morally and spiritually crucial issues. Even our knowing is something to be offered to God, and thus the question of how we know must be approached in a Christ-honoring and submissive posture.

When we come to know, particularly know God, we are like children sitting on the Father's lap, and the fact that our brains work, that we can think, that we can make logical inferences, that we can articulate a coherent sentence, is due entirely to the grace of God.[6] He holds us and gives us the very ability to think, know, and speak about him, even if critically. Therefore, Augustine writes, "There is no effrontery in burning to know, out of faithful piety, the divine and inexpressible truth that is above us, provided the mind is fired by the grace of our creator and savior, and not inflated by

---

[6]The image of a child sitting on a father's lap and striking the father who holds the child is from the Dutch philosopher and apologist Cornelius Van Til.

arrogant confidence in its own powers."[7] We should strive for knowledge, particularly knowledge of God, but always with full recognition that the *only* reason we can think rightly of God is that our minds have been "fired" by God's grace.

Paul's warning in 1 Corinthians 8:1–2 is a reminder that whenever we come to know something, our very capacity to know is brought about and sustained—*in every instance*—by God. There is therefore no room for boasting. Knowledge, for the Christian, should never puff up.

In 2 Timothy Paul makes an intriguing comment. He is writing about what the "Lord's servant" (a pastor, elder, bishop) must be like.

> And the Lord's servant must not be quarrelsome but kind to everyone, able to teach, patiently enduring evil, correcting his opponents with gentleness. God may perhaps grant them repentance leading to a knowledge of the truth, and they may come to their senses and escape from the snare of the devil, after being captured by him to do his will. (2 Tim. 2:24–26)

Notice the connection Paul makes between repentance and knowledge of the truth. If the Christian pastor is not quarrelsome but is kind to everyone, is able to teach, patiently endures evil, and corrects opponents with gentleness, then God might work in this person's ministry to bring his "opponents" to repentance, and thus to a knowledge of the truth. With such knowledge of the truth they may "come to their senses and escape the snare of the devil," having been previously "captured by him to do his will."

What is intriguing is that, at one level, a knowledge of the truth proceeds through the path of repentance. It may indeed be that—following Paul—to truly know cer-

---

[7]Augustine, *The Trinity*, trans. Edmund Hill, The Works of Saint Augustine (Brooklyn, NY: New City, 1991), 5.1.

THE GOSPEL AND THE MIND

tain things (all things?) involves repentance. Paul himself presents a type of "faith seeking understanding" that is in full agreement with passages like Proverbs 1:7, "The fear of the LORD is the beginning of knowledge." But another insight may be missed if we generalize too quickly. Paul is writing explicitly to pastors. He is giving instructions as to how to conduct their ministry. And the people who may be led to repentance, be led to a knowledge of the truth, come to their senses, and escape the Evil One's machinations are people who benefit from a particular kind of pastoral ministry. This means that learning, education, and knowledge in the fuller sense of those terms comes about only for those who are meaningfully involved in the life of the Christian church.

It is easy to miss this, since we often read a passage of the Bible with a view toward particular applications. But we should not overlook the obvious: God has chosen to change lives and work in his people through the local church and the ministry of pastors. To put it plainly: to truly have a Christian mind, to truly be a Christian intellectual, is to have a mind transformed by Christ. And to have a mind transformed by Christ—a mind moved to repentance, led to knowledge of the truth, and able to escape the snare of the Devil—is to have placed oneself within a key channel of grace, a church where biblical pastoral ministry is practiced.

Other portions of Scripture treat faith and obedience as inseparable. For example, in Revelation 12:17 the Serpent or dragon (the Evil One and/or his minions) is engaged in conflict with the woman and her descendents (the church or people of God). The dragon makes war on "those who keep the commandments of God and hold to the testimony of Jesus." The phrases "keep the commandments of God" and "hold to the testimony of Jesus"—if not synonymous—at least describe the same people. That is, to believe in Jesus is in fact to keep God's commands. Just two chapters later, John speaks of "those who keep the commandments of God and their faith in Jesus" (Rev. 14:12). Again, keeping God's commands and having faith in Jesus clearly describe the same group of people.

Creaturely Knowing by Grace

To know God is to honor him, as Calvin suggests. Why is this the case? In knowing God, we are knowing someone who is personal, a triune personal being. We are knowing more than this or that fact. We are involved in an interpersonal relationship. As C. S. Lewis reminds us in his book on the Psalms, "There is no question of learning a subject but of steeping ourselves in a Personality, acquiring a new outlook and temper, breathing a new atmosphere, suffering Him, in His own way, to rebuild in us the defaced image of Himself."[8]

When we know God, we know him on his terms. We know him by using the brains he provides. The act of saying we know God uses the vocal chords he has made and the oxygen he supplies. To echo Cornelius Van Til, we are like children sitting in their daddy's lap saying, "I believe in you." And when people deny belief in God, they are also like children sitting in their daddy's lap, in that he sustains every ounce of their existence. God even provides the brains, vocal chords, and oxygen necessary when the ungrateful person says, "I don't believe God exists."

All this is to say that knowledge of God is personal and ultimately moral. That is, to live in this world is—from the earliest moments of our existence—to face a moral responsibility and duty. If, as we have seen, God has revealed himself

---

[8]C. S. Lewis, *Reflection on the Psalms* (1958; repr., Glasgow: Fontana, 1964), 95–96.

to all persons through the created order, then *all persons know God and are engaged in the moral, willful, ethical submission to or rejection of the God of Holy Scripture at virtually all moments of their existence.*

The Inescapability of the Moral Nature of Knowledge

Someone might argue at this point: "Fine, knowledge *of God* has this moral component and may require a moral and ethical response—we must honor God if we really claim to know him—but certainly knowledge *more generally* is neutral and doesn't have such a moral or ethical component." This argument might hold if we served a deistic God—one who created the world and then effectively vacated the premises. But the God of Christianity not only *created* the world. The God of Christianity created the world through the Son—creation is christocentric—and now *rules, governs,* and *sustains* the created order, guiding it to its appointed end. Thus, nothing can be *truly* understood unless it is understood *in relation to the God who created and currently sustains the world.*

For example, as I look outside my window right now while sitting at desk 13 at Tyndale House in Cambridge, England, I see a tree. The tree is around fifty feet tall and has small oblong green leaves. If I am not careful, I might say that the tree is most essentially a wooden thing that grows in England and sprouts leaves. I might add that this tree has been created by God, is sustained by God, and in its own unique and mysterious way testifies to the creativity of God and is a conduit through which God reveals something of himself. And that is the temptation: to think of the notion that the tree is created and sustained and revelatory as an extra and nonessential part. We should rather say that the fact that the tree is created, sustained, and revelatory is utterly central to what this tree is, and to ignore this is fundamentally to misunderstand what the tree is and to have a truncated knowledge of the tree.

To know something truly is to know it as it is understood and known by God. Certainly we created beings do not know the way God knows. Our knowledge is limited—we do not have the gift of omniscience. However, as created beings we can know the created order *in the light of who God is and what he has spoken.* In short, we can "think God's thoughts after him" (Kepler) without claiming omniscience.

Thus, even in knowing the created order, there is still a moral and ethical component to our knowledge because it is incumbent on us to know and understand things in the light of who God is and what he has spoken. We must assent to God's understanding of things if our knowledge is to be in accord with what something really is. For example, the individual sharing a carrel with me is not simply an organism with two legs, two arms, and two eyes doing research in the area of New Testament. He is a created being, a man made in the image of God, a person who has been given gifts and is accountable to God for how those gifts are used, someone being sustained by God in every breath he takes and held together in every smidgeon of his existence, who will one day face God and give an account of his life. My carrel mate's createdness and status as a gifted image bearer, sustained and accountable to God, are not extra things added to his basic identity. These things are fundamental and essential to who he is.

Let us, however, be sure to avoid an unhelpful trajectory. At times in this book I have warned about being utilitarian or pragmatic about the intellectual quest. We should not be consumed with knowing immediately what to do with knowledge. Coming to know something can often be a joyous occasion in itself, and we need not always be figuring out what uses of knowledge may follow. I am thinking of the person who feels almost nervous or guilty about enjoying intellectual pursuits that do not seem practical or lead directly toward something like evangelism. We can affirm that learning is a gift from God and (following Augustine) is brought about because Christ is the "Teacher" illumining the human mind in every act of knowledge. We can say with C. S. Lewis, in "Learning in War-Time," that all knowing is, in a sense, for its own sake while also being ultimately for God's sake. We can enjoy reading a good book without in the back of our minds feeling guilty if we do not find a great illustration for sharing the gospel or we have not been thinking through how this wonderful book will help us in our next evangelistic encounter. I speak in somewhat exaggerated terms to make the point.

That point is that in all of our knowledge, we know as God's creatures, moral agents in God's world. All of our knowledge occurs because God is graciously sustaining us in all that we do and providing for us such that knowing can occur.

Knowing and the Nature of the Human Heart
Early in this chapter I quoted John Ruskin: "Modernism began and continues wherever civilisation began and continues to *deny* Christ."[9] Colin Gunton has written that modernity is "in need of the healing light of the gospel of the Son of God, made incarnate by the Holy Spirit for the perfecting of the creation."[10] What is intriguing about the Ruskin quotation is that he (rightly) draws attention to the relationship between (1) modernism (a movement or

---

[9]Ruskin, *Lectures on Architecture and Painting*, 157. Cf. Fuller, *Theoria*, 139.
[10]Gunton, *The One, the Three and the Many*, 1.

period of history often marked by a rejection of key tenets of historic Christianity and skepticism toward the possibility of knowing God) and (2) a culture's posture toward Christ himself. That is, Ruskin's pithy quotation suggests that modernism is fundamentally a movement rooted in the denial of Christ.

In Romans 1 Paul teaches that all persons, at some fundamental level, know God but *suppress* this knowledge. God has revealed himself through "the things that have been made" (i.e., the created order, v. 20). But people "by their unrighteousness suppress the truth," and God's wrath is being revealed against this ungodliness (v. 18). And note that this knowledge is not simply potential or possible. Paul is clear that what can be known about God "is plain to them" (v. 19), that "God has shown it to them" (v. 19), that even God's attributes (or some of them) "have been clearly perceived" (v. 20). The clarity and reality of the knowledge provide justification for what Paul says at the end of verse 20: "They are without excuse."

If people are "without excuse" on the basis of how they have responded to God's speech to them given in the created order, then clearly knowledge—at least of God—is fundamentally moral in nature. When God speaks we must respond. To suppress what God has spoken in the created order is like a child ignoring his father's clear directive. Man is morally accountable for what God has spoken to him.

Augustine, Knowledge, and Love
We have seen that Augustine brings much to the discussion of a Christian understanding of the intellectual life. In *The Trinity*, and elsewhere, he argues that one must *love* what one *knows*. The intellectual endeavor, the quest for

knowledge, is not simply about accumulating a storehouse of facts or, in today's cyber world, downloading data. The mind's pursuits are always, and without fail, related to one's "loves," or to the state of the heart. Thus, for Augustine, following Paul, we really cannot know what we do not love.

It is only when we love something that we can begin to grasp its true potential. That is, though this world is good, we do not recognize that goodness unless we appreciate that the world is headed somewhere. It is headed toward its ultimate purpose, a purpose about which we see hints in Genesis 1–2 and a fuller portrayal in the final chapters of Revelation.[11]

Love views something or someone in terms of the future. A loving parent listening to a child clunk out notes on the piano hears something greater than the discordant tones, bad rhythm, and heavy-handed attack that would assault a stranger's ears. The parent has a vision or hope (we might say an eschatological vision) of what the child is capable of and what might actually be the case one day.

Similarly, Augustine seems to be saying that the reason we can know only what we love is that only in love are we able to understand what something is really like in terms of what it is ultimately capable of becoming. This kind of love, which loves someone for what he or she *will* be, is surely what Augustine has in mind in *The Trinity* when he speaks of God's love for us: "It is through this faith that we come at last to sight, so that he may love us for actually being what he now loves us that we might be; and that we may no more be what he now hates us for being, and what he urges and helps us not to want to be for ever."[12]

---

[11] My thinking along these lines was originally prompted, I believe, by A. J. Conyers.
[12] Augustine *The Trinity* 1.21.

Similarly, speaking of someone's love for another person, Augustine writes, "True love then is that we should live justly by cleaving to the truth, and so for the love of men by which we wish them to live justly we should despise all mortal things."[13]

Augustine's emphasis on love helps us understand what a Christian intellectual life might look like. God is to be loved, while all other things are to be viewed in relation to that ultimate love: "Not all things, however, which are to be used are also to be loved, but only those which can be related to God together with ourselves in a kind of social companionship."[14] Rather than the intellectual life having simply an impersonal pragmatic or utilitarian end, Augustine can construe liberal arts as means by which man fulfills his ultimate destiny, which is to love.

Perhaps this is why reading Augustine is so much more joyous (at least for me) than reading much of modern thought. Augustine views education in explicitly love-drenched and love-driven terms. In reading an author closely, I am *loving* the author (even if deceased). Indeed, if I do not in some sense love the author, I will not show care for what he or she has said, and hence I will not understand the book. Thus, interpreting a book rightly requires the Christian virtue of love. And in teaching well I am loving my students, for God might just see fit to use a well-turned phrase or well-timed criticism to shape the student that much more into becoming all that he or she is destined to be under God.

Augustine helps us immensely, for he draws the intricate connection between knowing and loving, and thereby

---

[13]Ibid., 8.10.
[14]Augustine *On Christian Doctrine* 1.23 (*Teaching Christianity, The Works of Saint Augustine: A Translation for the 21st Century*, trans. Edmund Hill, ed. John E. Rotelle [Brooklyn, NY: New City, 1992]).

gives us insight into the connection of knowing to *doing*. Every introductory course in ethics raises the question of motivation for action. That is, even when someone knows something—for example, that one course of action is better than another—why does that person not always *act* on that knowledge? Put differently, even when someone knows something, what is it that then brings the person to act? It is a good question, and I am not sure that it can be answered apart from a Christian understanding of reality. What Augustine draws to our attention is that all of our decisions flow ultimately from the heart, or from our "loves." When our loves are disordered, or perverse, we act accordingly. Augustine helped Western Christendom hammer out the notion that all of life, the entire plan of history, is ultimately the outworking of two different loves: the love of self (in the narcissistic sense) and the love of God. These two loves characterize the two cities: the city of man and the city of God.

To say that knowledge is a *moral* reality related to our *hearts* is to say that it is a matter of our *wills*. As illustrated earlier, Augustine suggests that the world is truly a beautiful place. But why do some persons not see the beauty that is objectively there in the created order? The question remains relevant to the significant cognitive disorder in a post-Christian age.

Irish theologian Stephen Williams has explored the nature of knowledge—particularly in the modern world—in his book *Revelation and Reconciliation*.[15] Whereas it is common to try to make sense of modernity in terms of *epistemological* issues (How do we know? How can we be certain of what we know?) or *ontological* issues (What is

---

[15]Stephen N. Williams, *Revelation and Reconciliation: A Window on Modernity* (Cambridge: Cambridge University Press, 1995).

reality? Is it primarily one or many? Is reality an illusion?),
Williams sees modernity as also (perhaps primarily) rooted
in the nature of the human *will*. Modernity is fundamentally
a *moral* issue: "Western atheism [a mark of modernity] may
be understood as a spiritual movement of the soul as well
as intellectual movement of the mind."[16]

On Williams's understanding, to understand modernity
we must understand the centrality of the human will. This
focus on the human will is eminently biblical. Williams
writes, "The theology of the Reformers themselves consistently reminds us that the biblical drama is about the tragedy
of a world alienated and loved in spiritual rebellion, root
of our cognitive dysfunction."[17] Note that Williams is not
denying the importance of right thinking. The root of our
"cognitive dysfunction" is our spiritual rebellion. The reason
that some persons do not see what is there in created order
is that they hold on to fundamentally disordered loves.

Two Christian thinkers who captured the dynamic
outlined by Williams were Blaise Pascal (1623–1662) and
Søren Kierkegaard (1813–1855). Pascal was a French math-
ematician, physician, and Christian thinker whose *Pensées*
("thoughts") are still read today. He was particularly clear
about the centrality of Christ and the role of our wills and
hearts in the knowing process. Thus, Pascal wrote: "Those
who do not love truth excuse themselves on the ground
that it is disputed and that very many people deny it. Thus
their error is due to the fact that they love neither truth
nor charity, so they have no excuse."[18] Further: "The great-
ness of wisdom, which is nothing if it does not come from
God, is invisible to carnal and intellectual people. They

---

[16]Ibid., 8.
[17]Ibid., 173.
[18]Blaise Pascal, *Pensées*, trans. A. J. Krailsheimer (Harmondsworth: Penguin, 1966), 84.

are three orders differing in kind."[19] What is needed, Pascal contended, is to see all things through Jesus Christ. Apart from this, we would have no true knowledge. Hence, Pascal was a true Augustinian when he wrote:

> Not only do we only know God through Jesus Christ, but we only know ourselves through Jesus Christ; we only know life and death through Jesus Christ. Apart from Jesus Christ we cannot know the meaning of our life or our death, of God or of ourselves.
>
> Thus without Scripture, whose only object is Christ, we know nothing, and can see nothing but obscurity and confusion in the nature of God and in nature itself.[20]

Friedrich Nietzsche understood Pascal well when, despite disagreeing, he summarized Pascal as follows: "Our inability to know the truth is the consequence of our corruption, our moral decay."[21]

Søren Kierkegaard, a Danish theologian and philosopher, clearly perceived—like Williams—the moral nature of modernity's resistance to the God of Scripture:

> People try to persuade us that the objections against Christianity spring from doubt. The objections against Christianity spring from insubordination, the dislike of obedience, rebellion against all authority. As a result people have hitherto been beating the air in their struggle against objections, because they have fought intellectually with doubt instead of fighting morally with rebellion.[22]

---

[19]Ibid., 308.
[20]Ibid., 417.
[21]Friedrich Nietzsche, *The Will to Power*, trans. Walter Kaufmann and R. J. Hollingdale (New York: Vintage Books, 1968), 1.83.
[22]Søren Kierkegaard, *Works of Love*, ed. H. and E. Hong (New York: Harper and Row, 1962), 11, quoted in Williams, *Revelation and Reconciliation*, 6.

The twentieth-century Swiss theologian Karl Barth (1886–1968) is in the line of Pascal and Kierkegaard when he says:

> Fine and impressive reasons are given so that men in the modern world *can* no longer believe the teaching of Christianity in its traditional form, without a deliberate intention to deceive, but in fact because people no longer *want* to believe it. Man makes the opposition to older Christianity which had come about through his new moralism into a contrast between the modern and the obsolete presuppositions for cosmology and epistemology—in order to justify himself.[23]

In short, modern man does not believe in God because *he does not want* to believe in God. And Barth is particularly insightful when criticizing the prototypical modern, Friedrich Nietzsche. Barth writes of Nietzsche: "[That] everything should finally become a formal crusade against the cross, is not immediately apparent, but has to be learned and noted from a reading of Nietzsche. Yet it must be learned and noted if we are to understand him."[24] Indeed, as Williams suggests, modern man's "difficulties" with the God of biblical Christianity may just be less about this or that intellectual conundrum than about a deep resistance to the notion that as fallen beings we are *fundamentally in need of reconciliation.* We are beings who need to be rescued. We need atonement, and it must come from outside of us. This is humiliating indeed.

Calvin on Knowing and Honoring God

Calvin's construal of what it means to truly know God provided the impetus for this chapter. Knowledge in the mod-

---

[23] Karl Barth, *Protestant Theology in the Nineteenth Century: Its Background and History* (Grand Rapids: Eerdmans, 2002), 94.
[24] Karl Barth, *Church Dogmatics* (London: T&T Clark, 2004), 3.2 (237). I was led to this quotation by Williams, *Revelation and Reconciliation*, 80.

ern world is often severed from any inherent relationship to practice. A Christian understanding of the intellectual life, on the other hand, has virtually always affirmed the necessary and inseparable connection between knowledge and practice. As we noted earlier, Calvin writes that to know God is to honor him. Calvin does not say that we can have knowledge and then later act on it. If we do not honor God, we prove that we do not truly know him. This is a far cry from modern notions of knowledge.

The recovery of a theologically faithful construal of knowledge needs to resist the reductionistic construal found in the modern world, in favor of trajectories like that found in Calvin. The Genevan Reformer was not inventing something out of thin air. He was echoing biblical principles that pervade the Old and New Testaments.

Conclusion

It should be clear that every act of knowledge is a subset of the life of discipleship centered on God. As Robert Jenson has argued, "In that the gospel comes to speak of God, it affirmatively interprets the aspiration for truth's unity: if there is a God, all knowledge must finally be knowledge of him or his gifts."[25] It may be easier to think about knowing and honoring God than to think of the proper ethical and moral response to reading a train schedule. But the point remains: all knowledge is received knowledge and is to be considered in relation to the triune God of Scripture and what he has spoken to us.

Here, as in so many areas, Augustine is helpful. He could write that we both love other things and love God, but when we love things along with God, we always love those other things "for God's sake." In the prayerful words of *The*

---

[25]Robert W. Jenson, *Essays in Theology of Culture* (Grand Rapids: Eerdmans, 1995), 82.

Confessions, "He loves you less who together with you loves something which he does not love for your sake."[26] That is, we have many loves, but all of our love for things besides God should always be appropriately related to God himself. We should have—in Augustine's terms, "ordered loves," and the ordering finds its ultimate end in the God of Holy Scripture.

---

[26]Augustine, *Confessions*, trans. Henry Chadwick (Oxford: Oxford University Press, 1991), 10.29.40.

Epilogue

Why is it that wherever the gospel goes the academy follows? What does the gospel have to do with the mind? I have tried—across five major themes—to delineate something of the relationship between the Christian vision of God, man, and the world and the intellectual life. The two theses I have argued are:

1. The Christian vision of God, man, and the world provides the necessary precondition for the recovery of any meaningful intellectual life.
2. The Christian vision of God, man, and the world offers a particular, unique understanding of what the intellectual life might look like.

When we look at the five main themes of this book, we see that the Christian understanding of reality provides a coherent account of the possibility of the intellectual life. There is an inextricable connection between the gospel and the mind.

First, I suggested that a doctrine of creation provides a reason to attend to reality, since historically to believe in creation is to believe that we live in a real and ordered and good world. There is something *there* to be understood and studied, and reality is not simply an illusion. We also saw that there is an important corollary of the doctrine of creation—the centrality of history. For a number of reasons, including the affirmation that we live in a created world, the Christian faith encourages attention to history. At the heart of all of reality lies a series of events that make up the gospel. And this gospel—the death, burial, resurrection, and appearances of Jesus (1 Corinthians 15)—shapes all of human history. It is a past-tense reality that bears on all that follows. Hence at the heart of Christianity lies the impetus to be a people who regard the past as important to the present. Likewise, we saw that often in Scripture God's people are called to remember, to recall what God has spoken in the past as central to life in the present. Christians, in short, are a people who look both backward and forward.

Second, we noted that the premodern (and generally) Christian world was often shaped by a belief that there was a telos at the center of history. History is going somewhere, and so are we. All of life is animated by a goal. In Paul's terms, we will one day see God face-to-face, and "I shall know fully, even as I have been fully known" (1 Cor. 13:12). I maintained that this sense of a telos shaped premodern intellectual life in profound ways, for people knew that their intellectual deliberations had meaning and purpose, and that they were thinking and living in a world guided and governed toward an appointed end. With the loss of this sense of a telos in the modern world there has been a corresponding confusion in thought, for when the denial of a telos is taken to its natural and logical conclusion, it leads ultimately to nihilism.

Third, I contended that the cross is central to the life of the mind. On a biblical understanding, we live on this side of the fall, and sin marks all of who we are, including our intellect. The cross redeems not just part of us, but all of who we are. Thus, it is proper to explore the ways in which the atoning work of Christ relates to the life of the mind. I suggested that the atonement allows us to think God's thoughts after him, and to see the world in light of who God is and what he has spoken to us. It is a mistake to privilege the human mind as sequestered from the effects of sin. The work of Christ allows—and invites—us to approach the living God, and it is only through the atonement that we can understand both God and the created order. Indeed, *nullus intellectus sine cruce*: "There is no understanding without the cross."

Fourth, I jumped into the contemporary fray over the nature of language. These were perhaps the densest chapters in the book. The twentieth and twenty-first centuries have witnessed bewildering developments in the understanding of language. There have always been pockets of skepticism in the Western intellectual tradition, but trends like deconstructionism, I argued, were the full flowering of the modernist worldview applied to language. Rooted in nihilism, deconstruction denies the possibility of determinate meaning and indeed cuts the heart out of the possibility of meaningful language. I suggested—leaning heavily on Augustine—that a Christian understanding of reality provides a compelling and coherent account of language. We live in a world with a Word—the Logos, the second person of the Trinity—at the heart of all reality. Since God is a communicating being who has created us through a Word to be communicating beings, and since all things cohere in this Word, there is good reason to affirm the possibility of meaning in language. All language is spoken against the backdrop of the Word, and all language should find its ultimate end in the "transcendental signified"—the triune Creator and Redeemer and Word sender, God.

Fifth, I emphasized that on a Christian understanding there is a fundamentally, though often overlooked, moral component to knowledge, and that true knowledge includes within it an appropriate response. I took my cue from John Calvin that "our mind cannot apprehend God without rendering some honor to him." To know God is to honor him, and the honoring of God is not a peripheral addition to the knowledge of God; rather, honoring God actually helps constitute the knowledge of God itself. I stressed that knowing is a moral reality, and that our hearts and wills are bound up with our ability to know. Following Augustine, Hugh of St. Victor, and Pascal, I suggested that we ultimately do not know or "see" rightly when our loves are disordered (Augustine), or when the eye of our heart needs cleansing (Hugh), or when we do not approach all things through the reality of Jesus (Pascal). In short, all knowing is inextricably moral, and the only way to have our loves ordered rightly is through Christ.

What I have written is a type of *apologia* (defense) of the Christian faith—perhaps not in the traditional sense, but an *apologia* nonetheless. If what I am arguing is true, then the recovery of any sort of meaningful intellectual life will be rooted in Christ and the gospel. And this makes all the sense in the world. The God of the Christian Bible is a God who is personal, relational, triune, and rational. (I realize that the word *rational* needs the proper qualifications.) He is a God who is not primarily sensed or felt— although that is part of our experience—but *known*. Thus, the fundamental goodness of knowledge is at the heart of a Christian understanding of the intellectual life. This God, who is himself personal, relational, triune, and rational, has made a world, and this world reflects the one who made it. We humans as image bearers reflect God in a unique way (a truth about which there will be pressure to compromise in our day), but the world as a whole ultimately reflects the God who made it. And hence, the Christian faith encourages attention to the world, its structures, and its mysteries.

If what I am arguing is true, then the anti-intellectualism that sometimes marks traditional Christianity needs to be addressed. If the gospel has within it the resources to promote the life of the mind, why do we see anti-intellectualism in portions of the Christian church? I can only offer three brief comments here.

First, it is likely that some persons have been unfairly written off as anti-intellectuals. Christians should be slow to believe what the secular media tells us about this or that Christian group.

Second, much of what passes for intellectual sophistication in contemporary culture is—if we are honest—undeserving of that description. If the acquisition of true knowledge requires—as I have argued in this book—that our hearts and wills be properly ordered, then much of what passes for knowledge is not, in fact, true knowledge.

Third, a pastoral word: C. S. Lewis argued in "Learning in War-Time" that certain Christians are called—by vocation—to apply their minds in a sustained way to the intellectual life. Christians who engage in intensive study should never forget the Christian church.[1] Much like the

---

[1]C. S. Lewis, "Learning in War-Time," in *The Weight of Glory and Other Addresses* (Grand Rapids: Eerdmans, 1949).

Dúnedain in J. R. R. Tolkien's *Lord of the Rings*, who patiently and faithfully guarded the Shire (even though the hobbits were unaware of their presence), so Christians engaging in scholarship should consider the moral obligation of their task. We engage in the life of the mind—at least partially—because we have a moral obligation to help and indeed to protect other Christians as we are able.

As is often the case with writing, many things have been left unsaid, and inviting trails unexplored. We are finite beings, and time and space are limited. I have not explored in any detail the fascinating world of contemporary science, and an extremely important field it is. I have suggested, however, that all knowledge, at the end of the day, can only be accounted for with the insights provided by the Christian vision of God, man, and the world. I have not suggested that only Christians have knowledge, although I *have* said that a fuller knowledge requires minds and hearts transformed by Christ. I have argued that it is the Christian understanding of reality that can account for the possibility of the intellectual life.

We are pilgrims traveling to the celestial city, and like Christian in *The Pilgrim's Progress*, we encounter various challenges and dilemmas along the way. We are progressing to our ultimate destiny, where, as Paul says, we will see God face-to-face. We will know fully as we are fully known (1 Cor. 13:12), knowing God more than we do now, though never exhaustively. And that knowledge will always be a gracious gift, as is all of our current knowledge. We will enter into the heavenly city because of the life, death, burial, and resurrection of Jesus. We will one day see the face of God because we have been transformed by the cross of Jesus.

As pilgrims, we live in this "already-and-not-yet" age between the inauguration and consummation of the kingdom of God. We may see "dimly" now, but we are still called to see and to know both God and his world. We engage in intellectual deliberation not only with the confidence that knowing is consistent with the Christian faith, but also with an awareness that the Christian gospel itself—and the larger Christian vision of reality—can account for the possibility of any knowledge whatsoever. This should make us profoundly humble rather than proud. We are God's creatures, and we think and know and engage our minds on his terms. We know now with confidence that all of our intellectual efforts find their true and ultimate terminus in knowledge of God himself. Such knowledge is possible because we have been transformed by God's most gracious act on Calvary two thousand years ago.

General Index

183

Bible, the, eschatological focus
of, 68
Bloom, Allan, 21, 61
on classical education, 65–66
Boethius, 87
Bonaventure, 97–98
Boyd, Richard, 129
Bradbury, Ray, 15
Brave New World (Huxley),
15–16
Bunyan, John, 59

Calvin, John, 26, 89, 111, 147
on knowing and honoring
God, 171–72
on knowledge of God, 150–51,
161
Chesterton, G. K., 58, 58n4
Christian orthodoxy, historic,
33–34
Christian vision, of God and man,
12–14, 16, 20, 21, 23–25,
26, 39, 62–63, 75–76,
86–87, 104–5, 107, 114,
144, 175, 180
Christianity, 28, 32, 57, 72, 75,
122, 142n24, 147, 162,
165, 171, 176
compared with Gnosticism,
36–37
historic/traditional, 49, 142,
179
and the novel, 144–45
objections to, 170
See also Christians; faith,
Christian
Christians, 67, 139n, 179–80
centrality of the cross to,
84–85, 99–100
importance of the past and
memory to, 46–47, 49, 51,
176
and the intellectual life, 86–87
and logocentrism, 142–32,
142n24

and moral judgments, 106n5
transformation of through
conversion and redemp-
tion, 90–91
what they can learn from
deconstructionism, 146
City of God, The (Augustine), 72
Closing of the American Mind, The
(Bloom), 21, 65
Confessions (Augustine), 143, 173
Confucius, 64
Consolation of Philosophy, The
(Boethius), 87
Conyers, A. J., 53, 58, 60n7
on modernity, 59–60, 112
creation, 31–32, 47, 50–51, 59,
64, 67, 69, 71, 71n28, 90n,
111, 113, 115, 146, 152–
53, 175–76
centrality of, 32–39, 52, 176
christocentric nature of, 162
creation *ex nihilo*, 33–34
doctrine of, 26, 34n7, 35, 38
God's role in, 37–38, 136, 140
and history, 50–51, 81
humanity's animosity toward
the created order, 34
and language, 127–32
and the reception of truth, 35
telos of, 90n10
Crime and Punishment (Dostoevsky), 143
cross, the, 86–87, 99–100, 177
and the mind in the New Testament, 87–92

Daniélou, Jean, 32
Dante, 59
David, 155
de Broglie, Louis, 29
De sacramentis (Hugh of St. Vic-
tor), 96
*Decline of the Secular University,
The* (Sommerville), 19
deconstructionism, 116n29, 125,
146, 177

90–92, 95, 96, 99, 164,
172, 175–76, 178, 179, 180
centrality of to a Christian
understanding of the mind,
58, 66, 92, 95
as the historical reality that
shapes all of history, 45, 51,
52
of reconciliation, 92
See also intellectual life, and
the gospel
Green, Bradley G., 12–13
as a student and teacher,
14–15, 150
Gregory the Great, 53
Gunton, Colin E., 56n, 79, 90n,
129, 151, 164

Hannah, 154
history, 26, 31–32, 176
centrality of, 39–49
"narrativity" of, 23–24
Hobbes, Thomas, 57, 106, 106n5
Hobbit, The (Tolkien), 59
Hofstadter, Richard, 21
Holy Spirit, the, 126, 128, 164
Hugh of St. Victor, 95–96, 127,
178
on the knowledge of God and
spiritual transformation,
73–74n
on the theoretical arts, 96,
96n21
humans
as created beings, 37, 37n16
"suicidal impulse" of, 43–44
as "wordish" creatures, 104–6
Hume, David, 56
Huxley, Aldous, 15

incarnation, the, 93
Athanasius's on, 71
Augustine on the incarnate
Word, 133–34, 135–37,
136n

faith as incarnational, 41
importance/meaning of, 132–
37
Institutes of the Christian Religion
(Calvin), 111
structure of, 150
intellectual life, 17, 67, 76–77,
179
and the Christian vision of
God, man, and the world,
12–14, 16, 20, 21, 23–25,
26, 39, 62–63, 75–76,
86–87, 104–5, 107, 114,
144, 175, 180
Christ's rule over, 89–90
decline of, 20–21
emphasis on in the Western
world, 26
eschatological nature of, 70,
72–76
evangelical approach to, 12–13
and the gospel, 13, 58–59,
81–82
Origen's view of, 16–18
Western intellectual tradition
and the journey motif, 59
See also cross, the, and the
mind in the New Testa-
ment; Jesus Christ, and the
life of the mind in Christian history
*Intelligent Person's Guide to Mod-
ern Culture, An* (Scruton),
18–19, 63

Jameson, Frederic, 117n38
Jeffrey, David Lyle, 107–8, 123,
133n, 134, 143–44
Jenson, Robert W., 21, 49, 101,
172
on the liberal arts, 22–24,
23n26
Jesus Christ, 17, 27, 41–42, 51,
62, 75, 84, 92n11, 98, 126,
128, 134, 157, 160–61,
170, 178, 180

Scripture Index